FROM GRASS ROOTS TO GREAT NESS

13 RULES TO BUILD ICONIC BRANDS WITH COMMUNITY LED GROWTH

LLOYED LOBO

Published by Damn Gravity Media LLC, Chicago

DAMN GRAVITY
WWW.DAMNGRAVITY.COM

CONTENTS

THIS BOOK IS
DEDICATED TO ONE OF
MY CLOSEST FRIENDS
AND OG COMMUNITY
BUILDER, VASIL AZAROV,
FOUNDER OF
GROWTH BLAZERS,
WHO PASSED
AWAY IN 2022.

REST IN PEACE,
BROTHER.

"CONSISTENCY IS THE MAGIC INGREDIENT THAT TURNS SMALL ACTIONS INTO BIG ACHIEVEMENTS."

NEVER MEANT TO build a community. Especially not one the size of SaaStr, now the world's largest community for B2B SaaS and business software.

Back in 2012, I was just a SaaS founder with seller's remorse. After Adobe acquired my first company, Echo-Sign, I should have been celebrating. Instead, I couldn't shake the feeling of regret, or at least, lament. We had just hit a million dollars a month in revenue, growing 100 percent year-over-year with 120 percent net revenue retention, and we were firmly profitable. It's clear, in hindsight, that we had a rocket ship and should have kept growing independently. But this was the early days of SaaS. We didn't yet have the luxury of industry benchmarks or lessons learned from top IPOs and founders who'd been there in SaaS. When the offer came across our desk, it wasn't clear what to do. It was hard to say no.

In dealing with the void left from selling my company, I decided there should be better learnings from the SaaS industry—specifically real-world lessons from founders who have been there. At first, I shared my experiences in building, scaling, and selling my company. Maybe I could convince the next founders who really had something to stay the course and not sell. At the very least, it gave me a way to add value and be relevant. Later, it grew to be much more, with hundreds and hundreds of the best sharing their own top mistakes and learnings on the path to success.

SaaStr started with a goal to write a hundred blog posts. From the very first article, I knew I had discovered an untapped market. Industry leaders like Stewart Butterfield (Slack) and Aaron Levie (Box) started commenting on and sharing my posts. My audience grew rapidly with every article. I was also active on Quora at the time, which drove even more attention to my writing. I wrote a hundred articles. Then two hundred. Brick-by-brick, day-by-day, SaaStr became the go-to resource for the B2B SaaS industry. It wasn't yet a community, but I saw an opportunity: to not just help fellow SaaS founders, but build a legacy for my old EchoSign team.

What they don't tell you about selling your company is that almost as soon as you're acquired, people forget you existed. My team deserved all the credit and opportunities in the world for what we built, but no one would ever know. If I could share what we learned at EchoSign, they would have a springboard for their next adventure. In the end, I'm most proud of the impact my small team had on the greater SaaS movement. We spun off CROs, heads of sales, and executives at unicorns like Gong, Brex, Rippling, and many more.

Even though I didn't at first mean to build a community, SaaStr always contained the nucleus of one: a passionate commitment to helping others. I believe our early followers felt this passion, not only from me but from other readers who left comments on my articles and replied to my Quora answers. Soon, people were asking me to organize a meetup, so I did. Over four hundred folks attended the first SaaStr event, driven entirely by our blog and word of mouth. Then we held a second event for eight hundred and brought in a few successful VPs of sales and marketing to share their stories. In 2015, we held the first SaaStr Annual Conference (it was bold of us to say "Annual" since it was the first one) for over 1,200. We've been going strong ever since.

I met Lloyed shortly after the first SaaStr Conference. He was building a SaaS startup, Boast.AI, while also running a community for tech founders called Traction. Always persistent, Lloyed followed up numerous times before I agreed to interview Ryan Smith, founder and CEO of Qualtrics, at Traction Conf SF. The event did not disappoint, and neither did Lloyed. He was a real-deal founder who attracted a like-minded and generous community. A year later, Lloyed volunteered to run an 800-person SaaStr event for GTM (go-to-market) professionals after our host dropped out at the last minute. Lloyed has never stopped being helpful and kind over the years. That's why I was more than willing to write the foreword for his book, *From Grassroots to Greatness*.

Believe it or not, we didn't start calling SaaStr a community until 2018. During a (much-needed) website redesign that year, I came up with the new slogan off the top of my head, "The world's largest B2B SaaS community." Some of my teammates pushed back and said we should call ourselves a media company instead. The term *community* was not widely used outside paid membership groups and religious organizations. How times have changed!

Today, community is one of the leading go-to-market motions in SaaS and beyond. Every company, large and small, wants raving fans who show up to events in droves. They want a brand that's not just respected, but beloved and iconic. They want to not just launch products, but change the world. And the best way to do that is with a small (or not so small) group of passionate advocates—a community.

If that's your goal too, you've picked up the right book. Lloyed is not only an experienced community builder, he's also a student of the craft, and I believe the best students make the best teachers. As you'll see in this book, Lloyed has soaked up lessons from the best communities in the world and put them into practice at Traction and beyond.

For the foreword, Lloyed asked me to share some key lessons on building community. I'm honored and happy to do so, but let me start by acknowledging there are many ways to build a strong community. I can only speak from my experience running SaaStr. One of my core beliefs is that you need to play to your strengths and passions, so take these words as inspiration, but forge your own path.

When building a community—whether it's an independent group or one to support your business—first figure out what type of community to build. That's where it's vital to know your ideal customer persona (ICP). What type of experience are they looking for: a place to learn or a place to unwind? What are their biggest challenges, and how can you address them? What other communities, platforms, or media outlets already exist to serve your ICP, and how can you offer something unique? Whatever you decide, be intentional about what you're trying to achieve and for whom. SaaStr grew organically, but we were deliberate about each step, from writing a hundred blog posts to expanding to Europe and Asia.

Next, ask yourself this first principle question: where can you add the most value for your customers and members? Most community builders make the mistake of starting with their own benefit in mind. This leads to overly promotional and over-monetized groups. Communities like this also lack staying power, because when times get tough (and they always do), their leaders move on to the next hot marketing trend. If you're serious about building a thriving community, you must ask this question earnestly and be open to answers you might not want to hear. Maybe you learn that community is *not* what your customers need, and that's ok. You just saved yourself a lot of time and effort.

Pay attention to when people start telling their friends about you. That's when you know you're on the right track. SaaStr was the only game in town for the first few years, so SaaS founders devoured our content and shared it with their networks. The product-market fit (or community-market fit, as Lloyed calls it) was instantaneous. But growth is often slow at first, so be patient. Show up daily to engage with your early members. Experiment with different types of content, events, and programming. Keep what works and throw out what doesn't. Consistency is the magic ingredient that turns small actions into big achievements, like compound interest for success.

Double down on what works, but don't let the member experience get stale. Keep injecting fresh blood into your community. We have a rule at SaaStr: add one small piece of value and one big piece of value every year. For example, we recently started hosting Workshop Wednesdays, a free, weekly masterclass taught by experienced SaaS leaders. Our vision for these events is a mini SaaStr breakout session from the comfort of your home. Like a SaaS product, you need to keep adding features and fixing bugs, otherwise your growth will stall and competitors will catch up. Find ways to attract new members and keep them coming back.

Be open about your missteps and learn from them. For SaaStr, running a coworking space in San Francisco was one that *almost* worked. We had some incredible teams in that building, including several future unicorns, but it only provided value to a relatively small group of people. That might be ok for some communities, but with a goal to be the largest B2B SaaS community, an effort that only helped a few was not fully aligned with our mission.

Lastly, remember this: whatever you choose to do, be the very best at it. Bad news travels fast, and mediocre experiences will sink your community before you know what hit you. If you're going to host events, go above and beyond to make them great. If you're creating content, make it the best thing your members consume that week. Don't just copy another community's playbook and recreate a subpar version of it. And please, think long and hard before you try to replicate SaaStr's event model. Frankly, I wouldn't advise anyone to spend $10 million and sixteen months planning a single event like we do for SaaStr Annual. Small, inexpensive, highly curated events are more accessible and just as meaningful. Again, only do things you're passionate about, because this is all too hard to do otherwise.

As your community grows (and I have no doubt it will after you read this book), don't get too caught up in the raw numbers. Bigger is not always better. When in doubt, go back to the first principle question: how can you provide the most value to your customers and members? If you can answer that question every day, week, and year, you'll be just fine.

Good luck, and remember to always be kind.

JASON LEMKIN
Founder, SaaStr
Co-author, *From Impossible to Inevitable:*
How SaaS and Other Hyper-Growth
Companies Create Predictable Revenue

GOOD LUCK, AND
REMEMBER TO
ALWAYS BE KIND.

JASON LEMKIN

"IF YOU BUILD A COMMUNITY, YOU WON'T BECOME A COMMODITY."

THE WORLD SMELLED like burning diesel fuel. As our old school bus lurched down the road, I kept my eyes glued to the window. Buildings destroyed, streets torn up, and vehicles completely engulfed in flames. This school bus represented our one and only chance of survival. I was just eight years old.

A few months earlier, Saddam Hussein had begun a hostile takeover of my home country of Kuwait in what became known as the Persian Gulf War. Danger grew by the day as Iraqi forces overwhelmed the small Kuwaiti army. Countries around the world prepared a response to the aggression, but for those of us on the ground, help felt like a million miles away.

Eventually, the war reached our front door. I remember my mom waking me up one morning and saying, "I don't think you can go to school anymore." We had to leave but still didn't know where we'd go or how we'd get there. (Being a fourth grader, I was actually excited by this news at first. I was sure I had failed a geography test after studying for what I thought was supposed to be a math test, and now my parents would never find out. God bless children.)

My parents were Indian expats who moved to Kuwait for work opportunities. Now their new home was under siege. Cut off from basic needs and utilities, our apartment building had to fend for itself. Elders, including my parents, pooled what little resources they had to secure food and water while waiting for the evacuation plan. Adults took turns guarding the building from looters and soldiers. Phone lines were cut, so news was passed by word of mouth from building to building. We took in other refugees who weren't as lucky as we were—their homes had been completely destroyed. Each building became its own small, self-sustaining city.

My family and I hunkered down in our building for several weeks while the Indian government figured out how to get us out of the country. Finally, we got good news: they had evacuation planes ready for us. The problem? They were in Jordan, a multi-day bus ride away. Worst of all, the only route was through enemy Iraq. Loading onto the bus, we were all nervous to leave the safety and familiarity of our fortified apartment building. But this was our only hope. We rode up Highway 80 toward Baghdad—what journalists would later dub the Highway of Death—dodging burnt-out vehicles along the road. Hundreds of people had just died in bombings there. We all feared the worst.

But then something amazing happened. A few passengers on my bus began to sing.

It started slowly at first, but soon, the entire bus joined in. Including me. People laughed and clapped with the music. Surrounded by war, we sang. It's a scene that will be etched into my memory forever. I realized something in that moment:

Life's not about the destination, nor the journey. It's your companions who matter the most. The people traveling down the road with you.

We were placed in a refugee camp outside Amman, Jordan. The UN dropped canned tuna and pita for us to eat. After nearly a week, we were finally able to board a plane to India. My family and I returned to Kuwait a year later, but seeking a more stable life, we eventually immigrated to Canada.

Even after the danger of war had passed, I couldn't shake that profound feeling I experienced on the bus. It's clear to me now, as a multi-time entrepreneur and founder of a 100,000-person startup community, that I've been chasing this feeling ever since.

The stakes aren't as high for me today as they were in those fateful days in Kuwait, but my purpose is the same: to bring people together to create impact and joy. Community has the power to transform businesses and the lives they touch. In this book, I'll show you how to harness that power to change your corner of the world.

Luckily, you picked up this book at the perfect time. Things are getting dicey.

THE RISING COSTS OF DOING BUSINESS

It's harder than ever to build a great business. What worked in the past is no longer working. The cards are stacked against you. There are numerous challenges, but here are the biggest.

First, customers are inundated by advertising—every minute of every day. Marketing has reached its peak efficiency, thanks to the power of the internet and big data. Ads follow us around the web, our eyeballs tracked across the screen, and our desires thoroughly exploited for another dollar. In fact, we're so overloaded by marketing messages that their effects are starting to wear off. Buyers are more educated, and more skeptical, than ever before. We've been misled by clever ad campaigns and pushy salespeople one too many times. Customer satisfaction across the economy is at an all-time low. Consumer trust has rightfully wavered.

In response, every company on Earth is trying to build an "authentic" brand to grab attention. They try to get a snarky Tweet to go viral to show they have personality. They greenwash their image to appeal to young people (as if consumers can't see right through it). Ironically, in their effort to be authentic, every company now looks and acts the same.

Second, even if you did find a way to cut through the noise, the cost of reaching your audience has skyrocketed. Every major platform, from Google to Meta to TikTok to LinkedIn, is throttling your organic reach. One dramatic example of this is Nas Daily, one of the largest Facebook channels in the world. In 2016, Nuseir Yassin started documenting his travels around the world through one-minute videos, eventually creating 2,000 videos and building an audience of over 21 million followers over 7 years. Each video reached over 50% of Nas Daily's audience. But as of 2023, the game has changed. Nas Daily's Facebook videos now reach just 5% of his followers.

If you want traffic, you're going to have to pay for it, yet even this is a losing strategy. For most growing businesses, digital marketing channels are becoming increasingly inefficient and unsustainable. In 2022, Insider.com reported that Meta's cost per thousand (CPM) ad prices increased by 61% year-over-year. But that's nothing—TikTok's CPM went up by 185%.

Although social media is a great way to discover new audiences and grow your network, depending entirely on it to build a business can be quite risky. Nas Daily's Facebook revenue took a massive nosedive from $100k per month to less than $3k per month. That's why it's crucial to have direct access to your audience through emails and phone numbers, and to actively engage with them off social media platforms and in real life.

Marketing costs and efficacy are just the beginning of the problems for businesses today. The way we buy products and services has fundamentally changed. People don't trust celebrity endorsements or AAA ratings from the BBB (Better Business Bureau) like they used to. Instead, we take the advice of friends and trusted influencers. Word-of-mouth is the most potent force in marketing. This is also happening on the B2B side of things. Companies don't sell directly into the C-suite anymore. Today, it's the end users who find, try, and buy products and services.

The terms B2C and B2B no longer apply. Today, every sale is person-to-person.

Many companies are trying to innovate their way out of the noise. It's why R&D budgets are higher than ever, and why I started a tech company that helps companies find and apply for R&D tax credits and funding. This works, but only up to a point. Great products that solve real problems will always be important, but technology advances are happening faster than ever. Today's cutting-edge product becomes tomorrow's industry standard, which becomes next year's outdated, off-the-shelf commodity.

In short, the old way of growing your business is becoming more expensive and less effective. Purchasing power has moved from the C-suite to everyday people. And with the increasing rate of innovation, it's harder than ever to keep up. While it's easier than ever to *start* a business, it's never been more challenging to grow and sustain one.

IF YOU BUILD A COMMUNITY, YOU WON'T BECOME A COMMODITY

But not every organization is struggling during these times. Some are thriving and growing faster than ever.

There are brands like Harley-Davidson, the 100-year-old motorcycle company that revived itself from the brink of bankruptcy. It did so by connecting riders to one another in their hometowns, and in the process changing what it means to be a biker. Today, people from all walks of life ride Harleys, from soccer moms to college students.

B2B tech companies like HubSpot and GitLab, despite fierce competition, have created entirely new categories and career paths. They remain on top by supporting their *industries* as a whole, not just their own businesses.

We see professional groups like Startup Grind, Physician Moms Group, Sales Hacker, and SaaStr, which have replaced the stodgy, often discriminatory social clubs of the past with welcoming, supportive, and purpose-driven memberships.

Finally, there are consumer companies like Apple, Red Bull, Duolingo, and Yelp, which have risen above the sameness of their industries to become icons of their age.

All of these companies are innovative in their own ways. All of them have marketing budgets. All of them have navigated the shift in purchasing power. But so have their competitors. Yet each one of these organizations has led their industry for years—sometimes decades. What makes them special?

In a highly competitive market, the most powerful and sustainable advantage you can build is a passionate community of customers, employees, and raving fans.

If you build a community, you won't become a commodity.

Community-led growth is the antidote to the problems faced by businesses today. It allows you to build real relationships with your current *and* potential customers. It not only insulates you from innovative competitors, it helps you lead your industry with cutting-edge insights from your market. Community is the key to building an iconic brand in an age of constant noise and churn.

On a deeper level, community-led growth improves the way we live and work. Humans crave connection and experiences, but our options for these things are dwindling. The more "friends" we collect on social media, the more isolated we feel. Our traditional community pillars are crumbling. We need a new breed of organizations that align with our purpose, vision, values, and goals. Brands and organizations have an opportunity to not only grow their bottom lines, but create beloved spaces for their people. Communities provide connection, autonomy, mastery, purpose, energy, and recognition—what I call the CAMPER framework—things we *all* need to lead a fulfilled life.

Together, we'll explore exactly what it means to be community led. But first, let me share how I developed the frameworks and steps that make up this book.

STUMBLING ON COMMUNITY-LED GROWTH

In 2012, after a series of startup "lessons" (another word for failures), I co-founded Boast.AI with my business partner and good friend from college, Alex Popa.

Our idea was simple: There were hundreds of millions of dollars of government R&D tax credits that went unclaimed; the application process was opaque and time consuming. Boast.AI set out to simplify R&D tax credits for technology companies. In doing so, we were helping fuel innovation that changed the world.

But we had a major problem: finding customers. Traditional sales and marketing tactics were extremely inefficient for us. Our market wasn't well defined or self-organizing. Companies didn't identify as "innovative startups looking for R&D tax credits." Most didn't even know these tax credits existed. Growing Boast.AI would require a massive outbound sales push and expensive paid ads to reach a broad business audience.

Or would it?

When you've been an entrepreneur for as long as I have, you learn that misery loves company. Startup founders gather not just to learn from each other, but to laugh, cry, and complain about the uniquely difficult challenge of building a business. Living in Calgary at the time, I realized there weren't many meetups or groups for founders to join, so Alex and I decided to start our own.

The meetups started small: pizza and pop in the community area of our coworking space on 14th Street NW. We invited every founder we knew and arranged a guest speaker—often another founder who had some modicum of success—to share some words of wisdom. Our early guests loved the events, and word began to spread. Month by month, the meetups grew.

Then one day, Boast.AI started to grow as well. Through our weekly pizza nights, Alex and I started meeting companies that could use Boast.AI's services. We weren't explicitly marketing or promoting ourselves, either. These connections happened naturally, which made them all the more powerful.

I didn't know it at the time, but this was the moment I discovered *community-led growth*.

Community-led growth is a go-to-market strategy that puts a community of fans, colleagues, and followers front and center of your business. It's more than an acquisition channel—a strong community is a force multiplier for every aspect of your business.

Our meetups continued to grow and eventually became an organization in itself. We called it Traction. We teamed up with another local entrepreneur named Ray Walia. Ray was the founder of Launch Academy, one of the largest tech incubators and accelerators in Canada (and also a nonprofit). The next year, we hosted our first Traction Conference in Vancouver (and almost burnt the stage down—more on that later).

As Traction grew, so did Boast.AI. The two organizations supported the same purpose: fuel innovation that changes the world. Boast.AI did this through R&D tax credits. Traction accomplished this by inspiring and educating technology founders. Today, Traction is home to over 110,000 entrepreneurs from around the world, where leaders from high growth companies like Atlassian, HubSpot, Calendly, Intercom, Zapier, and more share advice with up and comers.

But Traction wasn't just a growth channel for Boast. AI—it was also our best talent and fundraising channel. After bootstrapping Boast.AI to over eight figures in revenue, we decided to raise our first investment round. We accomplished this in a matter of weeks, and 100 percent through connections made at Traction. In the end, we secured over $100 million in venture capital and debt financing.

Community-led growth is not just a marketing tool you tack on to your existing business. It *becomes* your business. You're community-led from the top down, inside and out.

WHY READ *FROM GRASS-ROOTS TO GREATNESS?*

Amazing things happen when you achieve community-led growth.

You stop existing as just a business and become an iconic *brand*. You no longer have customers, but raving fans. People don't just recommend you; they get your logo tattooed on their bodies. You don't just become profitable; you make your little corner of the world—your community—a better place.

I wrote this book for anyone who believes in the power of bringing people together—specifically startup founders, CEOs, growth leaders, and community managers who want to harness the power of community-led growth.

Over the last decade, I've used the frameworks and rules in this book to help build multiple organizations. I've also studied some of the best communities in the world up close and personal—from small meetups to massive, international organizations like SaaStr. I hope to send you off in the right direction and avoid common mistakes.

When I talk to people about building a community for their business or cause, the first thing they ask me is, "Should I start a Facebook group or a Discord group?" This is the wrong question.

Instead, I encourage you to start with first principles.

"The normal way we conduct our lives is, we reason by analogy," said Elon Musk in a 2012 interview with Kevin Rose. "[With analogy] we are doing this because it's like something else that was done, or it is like what other people are doing. [With first principles] you boil things down to the most fundamental truths . . . and then reason up from there."

This book focuses on the first principles of community-led growth. I've distilled these principles down to thirteen rules:

RULE 1: Unleash CAMPER

RULE 2: Pick Your Community Model

RULE 3: Discover Your Why

RULE 4: Set an Inspiring Goal

RULE 5: Find Your People

RULE 6: Nail Then Scale

RULE 7: Create the "Aha" Moment

RULE 8: Design Unforgettable Experiences

RULE 9: Collaborate with Your Community

RULE 10: Reward Your Champions

RULE 11: Make Your Community Sticky

RULE 12: Show Up Consistently

RULE 13: Measure and Monetize

To illustrate each of these rules, we'll look at thriving community-led organizations from every industry: Apple, Atlassian, CrossFit, Duolingo, Gainsight, GitLab, Harley-Davidson, HubSpot, Knoetic, Peloton, Physician Moms Group, Red Bull, SaaStr, Sales Hacker, Startup Grind, Yelp, and more.

Along the way you'll hear from some of the foremost experts on community: Noah Kagan (Mint.com, AppSumo), Laura Nestler (Yelp and Duolingo), Joseph Quan (CPOHQ), Aradhna Krishna (Sensory Marketing Researcher at the University of Michigan), Derek Andersen (Startup Grind), Jason Lemkin (SaaStr), Anu Bharadwaj (Atlassian), Joseph Pine and James Gilmore (authors of *The Experience Economy*), Jonathan Yaffe (AnyRoad), Nick Mehta (Gainsight), Nuseir Yassin (Nas Daily) and others who have paved the way for you. You can't build community without a variety of voices and perspectives.

By the end of this book, you won't just have a framework for achieving community-led growth—you'll be so inspired by these stories that you *sprint* out of your office or home, out onto the street, and start building a community with the first people you meet.

The 13 rules are organized in a specific way and designed to build off each other. That's why I recommend you read the book all the way through at least once. This will give you a big-picture understanding of the community-led growth model. Once you're familiar with the concepts, feel free to jump around and return to different rule as necessary. Ready to grow? Flip to Rule 6: Nail Then Scale. Struggling with retention? Refer to

Rule 11: Make it Sticky. Losing motivation? Go back to Rule 3 and rediscover your Why.

This book is your manual for changing your business—and the world—through the power of community.

Now it's time to build.

BONUS CONTENT

Get more community-led growth tools, resources, and case studies by going to:

WWW.LLOYEDLOBO.COM/BONUS

RULE 1:
UNLEASH CAMPER

"CAMPER IS MORE THAN A SET OF IDEALS FOR YOUR COMMUNITY. IT HAS THE POWER TO CHANGE LIVES."

VANCOUVER, 2015. Standing backstage at our very first Traction Conf, I smelled smoke.

We were already at double capacity in the only venue we could find last minute: a seedy EDM nightclub downtown. (On the bright side, we had no shortage of purple, green, blue, and orange laser lights to shine on the enthusiastic crowd.) The thought of fire nearly gave me a heart attack. I frantically searched for the source of the smell.

Ray Walia, one of my Traction co-founders, was busy giving directions to his cousin who we hired to do the catering. Our next speaker was in the wings, preparing to run on stage, when she smelled the smoke too. The look we shared was surreal: a mix of surprise, concern, and the nervous excitement that comes just before giving a speech.

When I finally found the culprit, I was both relieved and mortified. Our smoke machine had run out of water and started overheating, searing the edges of the stage curtains next to it. The real smoke blended right in with the fake smoke (there's a lesson in there). *Who was supposed to refill the smoke machine?* It was a rhetorical question. Whose job would it be other than mine? A better question might be *why* we were using a smoke machine in the first place.

To fill the speaker lineup for our first conference, I sent a cold email to virtually every startup CEO in North America with a public email address. I thought only a handful would even respond, so when thirty of them said yes, I was ecstatic. And then I briefly panicked, because now our schedule was overbooked. That's when we decided to cut the standard thirty-minute keynote down to just fifteen minutes. To signal the end of each speaker's time, what did we do? You guessed it: we blasted them with the smoke machine. Not the brightest idea I've ever had.

With the smoke machine retired and crisis averted, I turned my attention back to the crowd. They were soaking up every minute. It was the most energizing startup event I had ever seen. We were onto something. No community event will be perfect, especially in the early days. And that's ok. Despite putting out multiple fires that day (literally and figuratively), our first event was a success. Even though the space was cramped, the talks were short, and the venue had a dancing pole center stage, our community didn't care.

Even that first messy version of Traction had the anatomy of a great community: CAMPER.

FORGET PERFECTION— UNLEASH CAMPER

Several years ago, I came across the work of business author, Daniel Pink. Pink started his career as the chief speechwriter for Vice President Al Gore and then went on to write five *New York Times* bestsellers. He's known for his unique insights on creativity, connection, and communication. When I picked up his book, *Drive: The Surprising Truth about What Motivates Us*, it couldn't have been better timing. I was striving to make Traction the best community for founders while also bootstrapping Boast. AI. I needed new ways to rally the troops and get us all moving toward a shared mission.

In *Drive*, Pink shares his three key factors for intrinsic motivation: autonomy, mastery, and purpose, or AMP for short. Instead of using the carrot-and-stick approach to motivation, Pink believes that leaders should help employees cultivate an internal drive by exploring their interests, learning new skills, and doing work they're truly passionate about. The AMP framework has helped thousands of businesses build more creative and innovative work cultures.

I was immediately hooked on the AMP framework and started experimenting with it at Boast.AI. We were always a very purpose-driven company, but now we tried giving my teams more leeway to develop creative solutions on their own. For example, we gave employees a small stipend for personal development, which they could use however they wanted. Our team loved it, and the work spoke for itself.

As our company thrived using AMP, I thought about how I could apply it to building Traction, because communities are built on intrinsic motivation. There are no sticks you can use on a voluntary group. And as Pink's research discovered, carrots are only motivating in the short term. Implementing the AMP framework was a great start, but I knew we could do more to build an enthusiastic, self-driven community.

My co-founders and I started talking to the founders in our community—why were they showing up to Traction meetups in the first place? Obviously, they all had the goal of building a successful startup. They were seeking *mastery* of the startup game, from managing their tech stack to hiring great people. But we dug deeper—why was startup success important? We learned that for many members, ambition came from the need for *autonomy* over their lives. They were intensely curious and wanted to pursue interests beyond what a normal job would allow. Financial success was just a means by which they could exercise that autonomy. On top of that, many were driven by a deep *purpose*, like supporting their families or slowing the effects of climate change. Traction helped them develop the skills needed to achieve that purpose.

But these weren't the most powerful motivators for our members. What really got people to show up—and come back—was the need for *connection*. Founders came to Traction to meet other founders. They formed friendships (and sometimes partnerships) that kept them coming back to each event. It became clear to us that great communities facilitated these connections. Additionally, when dozens of these connections were happening in the same room at the same time, it created a sense of *energy*—a feeling of progress, movement, and opportunity. A community without energy is like a body without a pulse.

But there was still something missing. Many communities had all of these attributes in spades, but they would fizzle out after a few months or years. What was the secret to sustaining a community for the long haul? I thought about my own experience building Traction. Ray, Alex, and I were committed to growing the community, but there was no way we could do it alone. Luckily, we had several superfans in the group who volunteered to help out. These rockstars were there to set up for events, welcome new members to the meetups, and give us unfiltered (and sometimes downright brutal) feedback on our content. They cared about Traction just as much as we did. Our superfans were intrinsically motivated to help, and we never took their support for granted. We rewarded them by making valuable introductions, supporting their career efforts, and recognizing them in front of the entire community.

And that was the final piece of the anatomy: *recognition*. Great communities rewarded their members by recognizing those who carried the load for the group. This not only encouraged participation, but sustained it for the long haul.

Building on the work of Daniel Pink, we developed a new framework for motivating and sustaining a thriving community: CAMPER.

+ Connection
+ Autonomy
+ Mastery
+ Purpose
+ Energy
+ Recognition

The nonnegotiable first rule of community-led growth is to build a thriving community. There are no shortcuts here, even if you think your community is a means to another end, like supporting a for-profit business. CAMPER is a sort of community rubric that tells you if you're on the right track.

Let's look more closely at each principle and look at examples from other communities.

TRAITS OF A GREAT COMMUNITY

CONNECTION
Creating relationships through shared values, experiences, interests, and goals.

AUTONOMY
Giving members the power to control their own destiny.

MASTERY
Facilitating personal growth and unlocking new achievements.

PURPOSE
Following a guiding principle, mission, and vision of the future.

ENERGY
Bringing movement, activity, and excitement to every experience.

RECOGNITION
Showing your appreciation for members and celebrating their success.

Inspired by the AMP framework from Daniel Pink

CONNECTION

Building a community is more than just bringing people together. You need to create connections between members through shared values, experiences, interests, and goals. Eventually, these connections become personal relationships, which serve as the muscles that hold the skeleton of the community together.

Connection happens more naturally in small groups. This is why large conferences have breakout sessions and group meals in between keynotes. The larger the community, the more important it is to give members small group time. Case in point: Harley-Davidson.

Harley is one of the world's most recognizable brands. It embodies the pioneering American spirit. But in the early 1980s, the iconic motorcycle brand was on its last breath. Low-priced motorcycle brands from overseas had flooded the American market, stealing away Harley's customer base. Motorcycles had become a commodity, so why would someone pay double or triple for a Harley-Davidson?

Despite their financial troubles, Harley still had passionate fans around the world. They needed a way to bring these people together. In 1983, the company introduced Harley Owners Groups, or HOGs for short. HOGs were local chapters that organized group rides, parties, and charity events. Motorcycle enthusiasts had always gone to a few national motorcycle events every year—like Sturgis and Daytona Beach—but for the first time, Harley riders had a reason to meet other riders in their city. For many members, the local HOG became the focal point of their social life.

Today, there are more than 1,400 HOG chapters around the world with more than a million total members. HOGs not only re-established Harley as the number one motorcycle brand in the world, but dramatically boosted its bottom line. According to the book *Brands and Branding*, HOG members spend on average 30 percent more than nonmembers on Harley gear and merchandise.

Pedaling in another direction, Peloton has used the principle of connection to create a virtual community of cycling enthusiasts. Peloton started when CEO John Foley wanted quicker workouts during his workday. Not having to commute to a packed class at a fitness studio meant he could have his proverbial "cake-flavored protein bar" and eat it too. It turns out he wasn't alone in that desire. Much like Harley-Davidson, Peloton created immersive experiences that turned solo riders into a community. Sweating and working out together, even virtually, led to a sense of accomplishment and camaraderie. Even in the years since the COVID-19 pandemic—when Peloton's popularity peaked—the community has stayed bonded to the brand. As of this writing, Peloton has over three million paying members.

Connection is never an accident. Like Harley-Davidson and Peloton, a community must intentionally bring its members together to create deeper relationships. One way to forge these bonds is by creating rituals. Your HOG group's weekend ride is a type of ritual. So is showing up every week for your favorite Peloton instructor (We'll discuss rituals more in Rule 11.)

There is no community without connection. Create intimate groups and allow your members to bond.

AUTONOMY

For thousands of years, philosophers have identified autonomy as critical to living a meaningful life. We humans need to feel in control of our lives, decisions, and direction. Successful communities give their members autonomy to "choose your own adventure" throughout the experience.

The most vibrant communities make autonomy a core principle. An excellent example is GitLab, the development, security, and operations platform for technology teams.

If I told you there was a multibillion–dollar software giant that had more volunteer developers than employees, you'd call me insane. But this is exactly what has happened at GitLab. GitLab relies on the open-source software community to build and maintain its systems. Over 2,500 volunteers make an average of 650 code contributions per month. As a result, the company ships software updates on the 22nd of each month, no matter what. This volunteer-driven, decentralized approach to development is a core principle of the open-source community as a whole.

How does GitLab balance this extreme level of autonomy with running a for-profit business? Most companies set policies to manage their teams. This is classic carrot-and-stick thinking. Instead, GitLab empowers its community with a detailed set of *processes*. GitLab maintains a 2,000-page company handbook that covers every aspect of the platform. It's a roadmap, not a rulebook, which gives members the freedom to build within the set guidelines of the company.

Does it take more work to give your members autonomy? Absolutely. But the alternate—command-and-control—will kill creativity, and ultimately, the community.

MASTERY

Mastery is the transcendent moment when a new skill "clicks." What started as an awkward and unfamiliar domain becomes second nature. Communities that enable mastery become central in the lives of their members.

Take Duolingo, the most popular language learning app in the world, for example. They've built their entire business model around mastery. Their goal is to not only help you learn a new language, but to eventually teach others. In 2017, Duolingo started language learning groups in cities around the world. If you lived in Denver and were taking Duolingo's Spanish course, you could meet up with other Spanish learners in your area to learn and teach. (These local communities are also shining examples of building connection, purpose, and energy.)

Another example is HubSpot, which has built a community of marketers, salespeople, and customer service professionals around the goal of mastering business growth. HubSpot has built a world-class online education portal where most of the content is free for users and nonusers alike. This commitment to education ensures HubSpot will never run out of qualified professionals to use their product.

Mastery is also the driving force behind your local running club, CrossFit gym, or outdoor yoga group. Each of these communities is built around self-improvement, in whatever form that takes. Some members of your Cross-Fit gym are training for the international CrossFit Games, while others are simply trying to stay healthy. Peloton, like many technology-powered fitness crazes, has gamified mastery to motivate users. Peloton members earn badges for reaching milestones like 100 rides (where you earn the Century badge) and participating in special workout events (like the World Mental Health Day ride). Plus, their rewards system is custom tailored for every rider. Yes, there are worldwide leaderboards, but even the average Peloton user feels like they are part of the race—the race to beat themselves each week. Personalized "Power Zone" challenges push riders to go beyond their self-defined limitations to become the healthiest, happiest versions of themselves.

Mastery looks different for every person. If you want your community members to love and rave about you forever, help them master their domain.

PURPOSE

Purpose is what separates a community from a crowd. Nothing is more powerful than a community with a strong purpose. As a founder and community leader, it's your job to beat the drum of your purpose day in and day out. Just when you get sick of hearing yourself talk about purpose, only then are your members starting to really pay attention.

Nick Mehta, the founder of Gainsight, has maintained the same purpose from day one: to prove you can win in business by being Human-First. Gainsight's aspirations go beyond the bottom line; they are trying to change the business world for the better. They built a community for all customer success professionals (not just Gainsight customers) called Pulse, which has become the living embodiment of this purpose. Pulse members come together to connect over business, community, and culture. Mehta reiterates the community's human-first approach to business in every keynote he gives.

Your purpose should scale as your community grows. When we started Traction, our purpose was simple: we wanted to grow while enabling others to grow, too. What started with pizza and pop has grown into a global community and conference. Our purpose now extends far beyond Boast.AI. We want to help innovators secure the funds they need to change the world. Every dollar spent on innovation returns twenty dollars to the economy, from vaccines to robots to clean drinking water.

A powerful purpose serves as the North Star for every decision and action within your community. I often think about the legendary story of President John F. Kennedy visiting the NASA headquarters. After a day of meetings that went late into the night, the president was walked out into the hall and saw a janitor sweeping. When he asked the janitor what he was doing working so late, the janitor smiled and said, "I'm putting a man on the moon."

That's the strength of purpose we should all aspire to build within our communities. Every task and every person is connected to the bigger goal.

ENERGY

Imagine this: You walk into a tan-and-gray conference room with a few dozen people standing awkwardly around the edges. The coffee is lukewarm and also burnt, somehow. The monotone murmur of conversation sounds like a swarm of gnats. Someone actually fell asleep sitting in a chair.

It wouldn't matter how much connection, autonomy, mastery, or sense of purpose this group had—you would bail on this event immediately. A community without energy is doomed to fail. It may never get off the ground at all.

When you think of high-energy communities, your mind probably goes to sports-focused groups like Red Bull, Peloton, or Lululemon. These are great examples, but in fact, every thriving community relies on energy to keep its members engaged. Sales Hacker, a community for B2B salespeople created by Max Altschuler, was built around energetic conversations in its online forum. To create this energy, Altschuler spent countless hours in the early days of Sales Hacker seeding conversations and commenting on user posts.

Apple is the epitome of energy. Steve Jobs showed us how to turn every product release into a global event, generating lines outside every Apple store in the world. Apple is one of the few thriving brick-and-mortar brands because they inspire people to not just *think* different, but *move* different. This energy is captured perfectly by Apple's iconic iPod and AirPod commercials.

Energy starts at the top. As a community leader, you need to model the type of activity and attitude you want to see. I'll show you specific ways to create energy in Rule 7 (Create the "Aha" Moment) and Rule 8 (Design Unforgettable Experiences).

RECOGNITION

Communities are voluntary by nature. Taking your members for granted is a surefire way to lose them forever. Simple forms of recognition are the best way to create superfans and evangelists.

Many communities have formal recognition programs, such as GitLab's Superhero program and HubSpot's Solutions Partner program. Other communities recognize their members informally, like giving them a shout-out in the group chat for helping another member. The best approach is to use both formal and informal recognition. Peer-to-peer recognition is particularly powerful and meaningful.

Recognition is the fuel that keeps your best community members going. In the future, they may not remember what exactly you said about them, but they'll remember how you made them feel: competent, appreciated, and loved.

THE POWER OF CAMPER

CAMPER is more than a set of ideals for every community. It has the power to change lives. It certainly changed mine.

After nearly a decade at Boast.AI, my co-founder, Alex Popa, and I sold a majority stake in the company and stepped down from our day-to-day roles, transitioning to the board. Virtually everyone in my life was surprised by the decision, including me. Boast.AI was my life. I had built my whole identity around the company. Now that

I had left the day-to-day, I felt lost. Clueless. The financial gain hardly softened the landing.

I wish I could say I handled the transition well . . . I didn't. I became insufferable, channeling my endless energy into all the wrong things. I started drinking more, going out with friends until wee hours of the morning, and eating junk food. I felt irritated with everyone, including my family, for no rhyme or reason, and little things would frustrate me to no end. In a matter of months, I had gone from being the co-founder and president of a startup valued at more than $200 million to rock bottom.

One day, my wife, Dr. Viveta Lobo, had finally had enough. She cornered me and told me to sit down. "The glass is always half full," she said. "You're fortunate enough to be in a position to do whatever you want. But by killing yourself, you're not only doing a disservice to your family, but also the community you worked so hard to build."

That was a huge wake-up call for me. If I wanted to be able to run around with my kids and fulfill my purpose of creating impact through community, I would first need to pick myself up and fix my health. Just like they say in plane safety demonstrations, your oxygen mask comes first. Life is a marathon, not a sprint.

The same day, I grabbed lunch with Atlassian's President, Anu Bharadwaj, in San Francisco. After sharing my sob story, she shared about her own struggles with losing her passion. After working in tech for twelve years,

Anu was burnt out. It got so bad that she went to her boss, the Co-CEO of Atlassian, to resign. "Don't quit," he told her. "Take the time off you need, then decide what you want to do."

This led Anu to taking the first sabbatical of her life. She spent an entire year fulfilling her longtime passion: wildlife conservation. She helped to rehabilitate lions and cheetahs in Africa and penguins in Antarctica. In between projects, she traveled the world. The break was exactly what she needed to get back on her feet. She returned to Atlassian happy and whole. As we said goodbye after lunch, she gave me one final piece of advice that hit me like a truck: "Self-care is never selfish. It is good stewardship toward the only way you can create impact in the world."

I couldn't sleep that night. As I lay in bed with these thoughts, I looked across my dark bedroom. In the corner, serving as a makeshift towel rack, was my old Peloton bike. I got out of bed, threw the clothes and towels to the side, and hopped on my first ride in years. Twenty minutes flew by like twenty seconds.

I'll remember that ride for the rest of my life. Starting the workout, I instantly felt a connection to the instructor, Robin Arzón. She began by sharing her postpartum lows, when she couldn't work out like her usual self. The song "Eye of the Tiger" was playing in the background. DUN . . . DUN DUN DUN . . . DUN DUN DUN . . . DUN DUN DUNNNNNNN. She told us self-pity is toxic. To defeat it, you just have to start with one. One rep, one step, one walk around the block, one crank. "I am, I can," she said. Those words coursed through my veins as I took the first crank of the pedals, then the next one, and the next one. I kept repeating the words. I am, I can. Best of all, despite riding in my bedroom in the middle of the night, I didn't feel alone. Seeing the riders on the sidebar made me feel like I was part of something bigger. Something meaningful.

That one ride turned into two. Then three. Before I knew it, I was on a two-week streak. I was completely hooked.

After so many months of feeling lost, I finally found something I could control again: my health. Peloton gave me a sense of autonomy over my transformation. With every ride, I cranked up the resistance and speed. My personal fitness tracker showed how much stronger and faster I was becoming. I was mastering the bike. Most importantly, those rides reminded me of my greater purpose—good health was the key to helping me run the marathon of family and community. Every ride energized me with music, the instructors' chants and words of encouragement, and the virtual high fives of the other riders. After every ride, Peloton would share the rewards, badges, and streaks I earned in recognition for my efforts.

Over time I started weight training, cleaning up my diet, and improving my sleep. "Eye of the Tiger" is still part of my morning ritual—when I wake up, after giving thanks for something good that happened the day before, I turn on the song and pump out as many pushups as I can.

The Peloton community picked me up and gave me a sense of direction again. All I can say is thank you to Peloton, and thank you Robin Arzón.

IT'S YOUR TURN TO BUILD CAMPER

Think about a community in your own life that has made you feel included, motivated, inspired, and eager to return. What was it that made it so special?

Chances are it embodied the CAMPER principles. It connected you to other members. Empowered you to choose your own adventure and master a new skill set. Pushed you toward a higher purpose. Energized you. Recognized you for your efforts. Maybe it changed your life, like Peloton did for me.

Now think about a community that didn't click with you. What was it that turned you away? Which CAMPER attributes did it lack?

The difference between a thriving community and a stagnant one is often subtle. Everything may seem fine on the surface, but dig deeper and you'll notice small mistakes that end up repelling members. Before, you may have chalked it up to bad luck or "competition." But with the CAMPER framework, you can evaluate exactly where a community is falling short and take steps to fix it.

If it isn't clear by now, let me say outright: Building a thriving CAMPER community is hard work. You have to be deeply in tune with your members, listen with empathy, and actively strive to improve every aspect of the experience. That's why, I believe, you have to love building community to do it well. If you treat it as just another job, it'll never work.

In the rest of this book, I'm going to teach you the strategies for building a thriving community and using it to fuel your business. But you have to supply the effort and motivation yourself. If you're not passionate about building community, I'd recommend a different growth strategy or finding a natural community-builder to help you.

That said, it's time to start, build, and scale your community. It all begins with choosing the type of community you want to create.

RULE 2:

PICK YOUR COMMUNITY MODEL

"WHEN YOU BUILD A COMMUNITY AROUND YOUR PRODUCTS, CUSTOMERS BECOME EVANGELISTS FOR YOUR BRAND."

WHEN STEVE JOBS and Steve Wozniak created the prototype for their first personal computer, the Apple I, they didn't unveil it to thousands of people. The big, flashy product launches came later in Apple's history. Instead, Jobs and Wozniak were surrounded by a few dozen computer tinkerers in a garage in Palo Alto—their fellow members of the Homebrew Computer Club.

In the 1970s, the Homebrew Computer Club was the place to be for Silicon Valley's earliest personal computer enthusiasts, the self-proclaimed geeks that spent their free time wiring up motherboards and dreaming of flashy new user interfaces. At their bi-weekly community meetings, members would bring their latest projects (or works in progress), share ideas, and help each other solve thorny problems.

This little community would eventually spark the PC revolution that would change the world.

The Apple founders weren't the only visionaries attracted to the Homebrew Computer Club. The club was a star-studded affair of early computer pioneers: Jerry Lawson, creator of the first cartridge-based video game; Steve Inness, primary designer of the early cell phone touchscreen; Ted Nelson, inventor of the computer back button; Liza Loop, an EdTech trailblazer who pioneered the use of computers for learning; Li-Chen Wang, an early developer of graphics software, including the program Palo Alto Tiny BASIC; Adam Osborne, creator of the Osborne 1, the world's first commercially successful portable computer; and many more.

What attracted all of these innovators to the Homebrew Computer Club? It wasn't just that they had a shared interest in technology. The club offered a kind of intellectual and creative safety that allowed its members to thrive. Instead of viewing each other as competition, they collaborated to bring their ideas to life. Members shared the belief that they were creating the future, and with each passing meeting, this seemed more true. So much of what we take for granted today—from smartphones to spreadsheets—can be traced back to this group.

Communities come in many shapes and styles. The Homebrew Computer Club is very different from the Harley Owners Groups, but they both embody the CAMPER principles: providing connection, autonomy, mastery, purpose, energy, and recognition to their members. What kind of community will you build? Let's look at your options.

COMMUNITIES OF PRACTICE, PRODUCT, AND PLAY

Why do people form communities in the first place? There are endless reasons. We are social creatures who will find any excuse to get together. Whether it's for safety and security—like my Kuwaiti community during the Persian Gulf War—or to usher in a technology revolution like the Homebrew Computer Club, communities bring people together around the things they care about most.

The goal of this book is to show you how to build a thriving business and iconic brand through community-led growth. To accomplish that, let's look at three community models that best fit that purpose:

+ Communities of practice
+ Communities of product
+ Communities of play

If you're building a community from scratch, it's important to choose which of these community models will work best for you. If you've already started growing your community, it will still be useful to identify which model you're following to refine your strategy.

COMMUNITIES OF PRACTICE: LEARNING TOGETHER

When Wozniak and Jobs joined the Homebrew Computer Club, they were looking for a group of like-minded technologists to help them grow as engineers and entrepreneurs. The Homebrew Computer Club was a community of practice: the primary goal was the exploration and mastery of computer technology.

Communities of practice help members develop skills, accelerate their careers, and explore their interests. They're focused on a specific domain, such as personal computers, rock climbing, B2B sales, or learning a new language. But communities of practice are so much more than classrooms—otherwise every school or online course would be a community. It's the social, peer-to-peer nature of communities that leads to connection and mastery. In fact, some researchers believe learning is fundamentally a social process. In a groundbreaking study, anthropologist Jean Lave and computer scientist Étienne Wenger discovered that when learners participate in "communities of practitioners," they connect ideas and activities more quickly. They call this process *peripheral participation.* This eventually leads to full participation, or mastery, of the domain.

In other words, by joining a community of practice—thereby surrounding yourself with newcomers, veterans, and everyone in between—you'll soak up learning and knowledge as if by osmosis. Communities of practice also provide a sense of purpose, energy, and recognition that don't always exist in traditional learning environments. Community keeps people showing up, and showing up is a prerequisite to mastery.

HubSpot has created one of the largest and most valuable communities of practice in the world. They do more than provide sales, marketing, and customer success education; HubSpot connects its users and encourages peer-to-peer learning. Their Solutions Partners program recognizes the very best marketers and agencies around the world, giving other HubSpot members examples to live up to.

What makes HubSpot a community of practice rather than a community of product is that their educational content extends beyond HubSpot products. By comparison, the Atlassian community is focused almost entirely on using the company's suite of tools more effectively (more on that next.) The key difference is *why* people show up: is it for the product itself, or for the larger domain and industry?

If people show up for your product or brand, then you have a community of product.

COMMUNITIES OF PRODUCT: TURNING CUSTOMERS INTO EVANGELISTS

When you build a community around your products, customers become evangelists for your brand. Let's look more closely at Atlassian as an example.

Atlassian is a publicly traded, multibillion-dollar company that builds productivity software for individuals and teams. Some of their tools, like Jira project management software, are the gold standard for the technology industry. Despite literally dozens of competitors over the years, Atlassian has maintained its leadership position thanks in large part to its community-led growth approach. With 3.9 million community members, Atlassian has one of the largest product communities in the world. They have local chapters on every continent except Antarctica, and many are extremely active. The Atlassian chapter in Cologne, Germany, for example, met forty-three times in 2021. Meanwhile, the Nairobi chapter had 3,382 RSVPs for thirty-three events! While the vast majority of Atlassian's community connects online, these in-person events are vital. They bring the most dedicated users together and create a deeper sense of connection for everyone involved—even those who can't attend.

Atlassian's community exists to help Atlassian customers do their best work. In doing so, they also infuse energy to a potentially dull topic. Community can change even the most mundane topics into something meaningful and exciting.

Communities of product can serve many functions for both the company and its users. David Spinks, the co-founder of CMX (a community for community builders) and author of *The Business of Belonging*, identified six key benefits of product-based communities. He calls them the SPACES framework:

+ Customer (S)upport
+ (P)roduct Development
+ Customer (A)cquisition
+ Customer (C)ontribution
+ (E)ngagement
+ Customer (S)uccess.

Communities of product are versatile and powerful, but they aren't the solution for everyone. Toward the end of this rule, I'll show you how to know if a community of product is right for you. But first, we need to cover one last type of community, and it's a blast.

COMMUNITY OF PLAY: HERE TO HAVE A GOOD TIME

Few brands are better at throwing a party than Red Bull.

Not just parties, either: extreme sports rallies, break-dancing competitions, concerts, downhill ice skating races, and a one-of-a-kind event called the Red Bull Flugtag, a competition in which amateur aerospace engineers create homemade flying machines and attempt to take flight (over a large body of water, for obvious reasons). Most teams fail miserably, but that's the point. For spectators and participants alike, everyone is just there to have a good time.

Communities of play embody the CAMPER principles in a unique way: the goal is just to have fun. The Red Bull Flugtag is a great example—these events are now held all over the world, *connecting* local communities around the ridiculous notion of testing out homemade aircraft. But there's a sense of *autonomy* in the fun as well: participants get to create a machine based on their wildest imaginations. What are they *mastering*, exactly? The art of the good time: dressing up, exciting the crowd, and going down in a watery blaze of glory. *Energy?* Well, it's Red Bull. Energy is their specialty. But what's the *purpose* of all this nonsense? Memories. Friendship. An experience you'll never forget.

Social sports clubs are also communities of play. Few players sign up to actually master the game of beach volleyball—they show up to have a good time with their friends. And for those who take the sport more seriously, there are competitive leagues and clubs.

Communities of play can be big business. If Red Bull isn't proof enough for you, ask the team at Barstool Sports how they're doing (hint: they were just purchased by PENN Entertainment for an undisclosed sum, but likely north of $500 million.) Despite their controversial founder, Barstool has built so much more than a media company. They've created a community of sports fans, gamblers, and good-time-havers around the world. Next time you walk around a college campus, look out for their iconic barstool and stars logo. You'll see it everywhere: on hats, on T-shirts, on lampposts, and maybe a few tattoos. You don't see people rocking ESPN or ABC swag. That's the power of community.

CHOOSING YOUR COMMUNITY MODEL

So now that you have an idea of the three main community models, how do you choose the right one for you?

When we started Traction back in 2015, our goal was to grow our R&D tax credit startup, Boast.AI. Why didn't we just build a community around Boast.AI, the way Atlassian did around their products? Communities of product are one of the most effective ways to grow and retain your customer base, but it comes with an important caveat: you must already have product-market fit.

Product-market fit (PMF) means you have a product that solves a problem *and* people are willing to pay for. Your customer engagement is high and churn is low. You've also found a business model that works at scale. PMF is a crucial milestone for every startup, and until you reach it, it's a bad idea to build a community of product.

Boast.AI didn't have product-market fit at the time. In fact, we barely had a product. We had found a burning pain point in helping startups apply for R&D credits, but we were still pulling a Wizard of Oz move by manually filing applications in the background as we built out the tech platform.

I still don't think Boast.AI could support a community of product, even after serving thousands of customers. Our product is fairly obscure and kind of boring (this is coming from a guy who obsesses over tax credits). Tax credits don't get people excited, and they aren't something founders think about often. Compared to Atlassian's suite of tools, which are used daily by entire organizations, Boast.AI is a product used once or twice a year at most. Customers love what we do, and we help them find millions of dollars, but there's not a huge need for product mastery.

That's why we created Traction as a community of practice that's dedicated to helping innovative founders change the world. We looked at the Why behind our product—why did startups want R&D funding and tax credits? We made Traction bigger than Boast.AI, attracting a wide range of entrepreneurs and technologists, many of whom would become Boast.AI customers, partners, funders, and employees. (More on finding your Why in the next rule.)

Did we ever consider making Traction a community of play? Not really. Trust me, we like to have a good time, but our focus is on helping innovators grow their businesses.

There are several criteria to consider when choosing your community model:

Product-Market Fit

Do you have it? If not, you're better off building a community of practice for your target market. You'll get to know your potential customers, their problems, and speed up the search for PMF.

This is how Joseph Quan grew his company, Knoetic, an HR analytics tool. To attract his ideal customers, Quan started CPOHQ, a community of practice for Chief People Officers. This community became an on-ramp for new Knoetic customers. It also grew Knoetic's total market as more and more companies saw the need for data-driven HR.

Frequency of Use

How often do your customers use your product? Are you part of their daily workflow, like Atlassian or Apple? Are you part of their favorite weekend activities, like Harley-Davidson? Or are you a beloved but less-frequently used tool, like Boast.AI? The more frequently your customers use your product, the more likely they will enjoy being part of a community of product. Otherwise, you should build a community of practice or a community of play around activities your customers do regularly, such as volleyball, startups, or inbound marketing.

Complexity

Red Bull is the most popular energy drink in the world. But the user experience couldn't be more simple: buy a can, pop the top, and drink up. Boast.AI's user experience is also simple: sign up for our service and we'll find you R&D tax credit opportunities and file on your behalf.

Simple use cases like these don't lend themselves to communities of product. On the other hand, Atlassian products are incredibly complex. They require communities of educators and seasoned users to help beginners. Other products, like those from Apple, are changing constantly, which encourages users to gather to discuss the latest updates and features.

If your product is complex or constantly evolving, it might make sense to have a community of product. This is why HubSpot has a product community in addition to its community of practice: to educate users and keep them updated on new features.

Market Maturity

In the early days of personal computing, there simply weren't enough users to fill communities of product.

Instead, communities of practice like the Homebrew Computer Club popped up to support the fledgling market. Microcomputing pioneers around the country worked together to create the personal computing industry.

Project management software, by comparison, is a mature market. There are millions of users around the world. More importantly, they know *why* they need to use project management software. Therefore, Atlassian's job is not to evangelize project management software as an industry, but to build a user base for their products specifically. (This is why, by 1986, the Homebrew Computer Club broke up. The industry reached a size where its members cared more about their own companies than the industry as a whole).

Notion has followed the same playbook as Atlassian. The relatively new project management tool, which was first released in 2016, has built a massive community of educators, enthusiasts, and evangelists around the world. The complexity of Notion's open-source model makes it ideal for a product-based community.

Like microcomputing pioneers of the 1970s, we see Web3 and cryptocurrency enthusiasts gathering in communities of practice rather than communities of product. These vanguards of technology are not just expanding the Web3 market—they are creating it. As the market matures, you can expect to see more product-based communities around specific tools.

Your Goals and Aspirations

Finally, consider what your personal and professional goals are for your community. Communities of product have a higher likelihood of attracting and retaining long-term customers, but they are naturally limited in their size. Communities of practice or play are only limited by the size of their market (and if your market is growing, your community growth is virtually limitless).

Communities of practice are also more flexible over the long term. By building Traction—a community of innovative founders—Ray, Alex, and I have a built-in audience for any number of new products or companies aimed at serving founders. In the same way, HubSpot can launch new products to their community because they serve more than just existing customers.

However, communities of product can rapidly establish your brand as the gold standard for your industry. Communities of product are the best way to turn customers into evangelists. If you recognize and empower them properly, you could be on your way to building the next Atlassian.

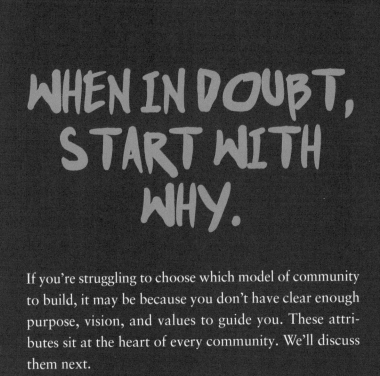

WHEN IN DOUBT, START WITH WHY.

If you're struggling to choose which model of community to build, it may be because you don't have clear enough purpose, vision, and values to guide you. These attributes sit at the heart of every community. We'll discuss them next.

RULE 3:

DISCOVER YOUR WHY

"A CLEAR VISION
DOESN'T JUST
GIVE YOU A SENSE
OF DIRECTION;
IT ATTRACTS
VISIONARIES."

DEREK ANDERSEN DIDN'T set out to create the premier global community for startups. He was just looking for a community to support entrepreneurship in his community. But now with 600 active chapters in 125 different countries, Startup Grind has unlocked a whole new level.

Andersen, who is also the founder of community-led events platform Bevy, has been running Startup Grind (SG) for over a decade. Today, the Startup Grind Global Conference attracts over 10,000 entrepreneurs from around the world. When he spoke at Traction Conf in 2019, Andersen shared a story about a pivotal moment in SG's growth. It wasn't a new marketing strategy or viral hack that elevated its trajectory. It was a clear set of community values.

Years ago, after a successful Startup Grind event, the keynote speaker whisked Andersen aside. The speaker was blown away by the enthusiasm and energy in the room. "Do you know why people enjoy Startup Grind so much?" he asked.

Andersen shrugged, but the speaker had a theory. "It's your values."

It was Startup Grind's commitment to friendship, giving, and helping others that appealed to so many founders who were jaded by the cutthroat world of Silicon Valley. "Yeah, of course that's what we're about," Andersen said. "Isn't it obvious?"

"It's not obvious," the speaker urged. If Andersen could make it crystal clear what the Startup Grind stood for, it would be like rocket fuel. That very night, Andersen wrote Startup Grind's first mission statement and added it to the homepage:

"We believe in making friends, not contacts. We believe in giving first, not taking. We believe in helping others before helping yourself."

Andersen calls SG's values "the most important piece of software we ever created." It wasn't software, of course, but the result was like adding a killer new feature. Founders from around the world started flocking to Startup Grind events. Not just any founders, either, but those who embodied SG's three core principles.

Many startups operate as if growth and revenue are their only purpose. This seems to work in good times, but when growth slows, these startups fall apart.

Community-led companies take a different path. They start with a clear purpose, vision, and values. They start with their Why.

START WITH WHY (COMMUNITY-LED GROWTH EDITION)

I'm sure you've heard the advice to "start with why." After Simon Sinek coined the phrase in the 2000s, it's been repeated so often that it's basically meaningless. But the kernel of truth is still there. When we break down Why into stages, it becomes a powerful tool for growing your business and community.

Community-led growth has the potential to sustain your business and brand for literally decades, even after you've moved on from the company. The real secret behind these companies is not their products or their brand, but a strong sense of Why they exist. This is the foundation upon which they build their community of raving fans.

Products drive cash flow. Brands drive profit. Whys drive movements.

In the previous rule, we talked about three different community models: communities of product, practice, and play. The community model is your skeleton. The Why is your heartbeat. Without it, your community will be lifeless, corporate, and transactional. Your Why attracts the right people and keeps your community headed in the right direction.

What does Why mean, exactly? Let's break it up into three parts:

+ Purpose
+ Vision
+ Values

Like Derek Andersen, many founders and community leaders assume their Why is obvious to everyone. This is rarely the case. Explicitly defining and sharing your Why is hard work, but it's absolutely crucial.

Let's find and build your Why, one step at a time:

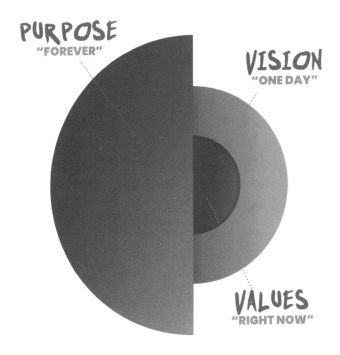

PURPOSE: WHY YOU EXIST

Your company's purpose is your forever goal. It's why you exist—your reason for being.

Map & Fire, an LA-based branding agency, shared my favorite definition of purpose:

> ## " PURPOSE IS A DRIVING FORCE THAT'S ALWAYS PRESENT REGARD-LESS OF WHAT YOUR BUSINESS ACHIEVES OR HOW LONG IT'S

AROUND. IT ACTS AS A NORTH STAR TO FOCUS EVERYTHING YOU DO. IT SHOULD BE A SOURCE OF INSPIRATION AND GUIDANCE THAT OUTLASTS ANY UPS, DOWNS, SHIFTS, OR PIVOTS.

Your purpose is bigger than you. It's even bigger than your company or community. It's a lifelong (sometimes multiple lives long) endeavor. At the same time, it's concrete enough to drive your decision-making.

Gainsight's purpose statement is both grand in scope and still actionable: "To prove you can win in business by being Human-First."

Gainsight championed a new organizational function called customer success, which helps companies reduce churn and grow recurring revenue by making customers *successful* with their products. Gainsight's business is a direct reflection of its highest purpose: they help companies win by putting their customers first! Strive for this level of alignment between your business and your Why.

A powerful purpose is something you work toward every day, but that work is never finished. There will never be a day when Gainsight says, "Ok, we officially won business! Time to stop being human-first." For Gainsight, the pursuit of their purpose is never-ending. It touches every part of their organization, from HR to product development to marketing. So far, Gainsight has been wildly successful in living their purpose, to the point where customer success has become ubiquitous in technology companies. They created a brand-new industry (complete with its own industry conference—more on that later).

Traction's purpose is to help innovators change the world. Our purpose has no end point—there will always be entrepreneurs and innovators to support. We know we're living our purpose when Traction community members raise money, sell their businesses, or partner with other members to build world-changing startups.

If your purpose has no end point, how can it be actionable? If you're asking yourself this question, you're still thinking about your purpose as a goal to achieve. Instead, use it like a compass to guide your decision-making. For Gainsight, the first and last question they ask themselves before making a decision is, "Does this make us Human-First?" If a business move would actually hurt their connection with their customers, employees, or community, it's an immediate *no*.

We follow this line of questioning at Traction as well. We ensure that every speaker we invite, venue we book, and piece of content we create is designed to support tech founders. If it doesn't, it's an easy no for us. For example, an expert in building food and beverage concepts once asked to speak at an event. We politely turned them down because our focus is on high-tech businesses.

A quick side note: some companies also define a company mission. Unlike a purpose, a mission is a lofty, long-term goal with a clear end point, like colonizing

Mars or ending world hunger. Some companies have both a purpose and a mission. There is no right or wrong answer here; it depends entirely on your community. Maybe a mission makes more sense for you. Go for it.

So how do you define your purpose? Start by answering these questions, and ask your leadership team to do the same:

+ What is your community's founding story?

+ Besides financial goals, why did you start your community?

+ What's a real-life story that exemplifies why your community exists?

+ Talk to five of your most enthusiastic customers or community members. Why do they keep coming back?

+ If you had to shut down your company or community and start over from scratch, what would be your purpose? (Many founders have a personal purpose that drives their entire career, not just their current company.)

VISION: WHERE YOU'RE GOING

Your vision is what you want the future to look like one day.

Community-led growth requires you to think beyond the next quarter, year, or even three years. A truly visionary community thinks five-plus years into the future and starts building that future today. Having a strong vision helps us picture the top of the mountain even when we're at the basecamp. It's motivating and also gives the community direction.

Joseph Quan, the founder of Knoetic (an HR analytics platform) started his community with a clear vision: to build the premier group for Heads of HR and Chief People Officers. He didn't care about being the biggest HR community. Instead, he focused on creating a group that would provide enormous value to CPOs—some of the busiest executives in the world.

This vision defined many of Quan's early decisions: who to admit (only the top HR executive at each company), what type of content and experiences to create (focused on HR strategy, benchmarks, playbooks, and CPO firesides), and even what growth metrics to measure (Weekly Active Users instead of Daily Users, because Heads of HR are too busy for daily engagement).

The result of this clearly defined vision is CPOHQ, which is now the number one community for Chief People Officers, boasting Heads of HR from Roblox, Glossier, Figma, and more.

A clear vision doesn't just give you a sense of direction; it attracts visionaries. If you want to attract high-trajectory people to join your community, set a clear and bold vision for them to fall in love with. Paint a picture of your ideal future and they'll help you create the path to get there.

The last benefit of a strong vision is that it forces ruthless prioritization. Recent research has found that without a clear direction, people will walk in circles—literally. A study dropped participants off in the middle of the Sahara Desert at night and told them to walk in a straight line. Even with the help of a digital GPS tracker, every participant ended up walking in a circle. Sometimes these circles were as tight as sixty-six yards in diameter. Our bodies make constant micro-adjustments in an effort to stay straight, but without a directional marker like a tree or the moon, we inevitably walk in circles.

There couldn't be a better metaphor for a community without a clear vision. If you don't know where you want to go, you'll make a string of micro-adjustments that end up spinning you in circles. Your vision is a critical filter for making decisions—just like your purpose.

Some founders start their companies and communities with a clear vision. If that's you, write it down and share it with the world. Your vision will attract visionaries who will help you get there faster. If you don't have a clear vision, that's ok. Start by answering these questions. You can also ask your best customers and community members for their opinion:

- If you perfectly executed your biggest dreams, how would people's lives be different? What would the world look like?

- Vividly describe your ideal future: What has become the norm for your industry? What problems no longer exist? What does it feel like in this future? Answer this question for twelve months out, three years out, and ten years out.

- Think about the furthest possible end point for your vision. What does it look like?

- What challenges have you faced in your life that you want to eliminate for the next generation?

VALUES: WHAT YOU DO EVERY DAY

Values are the way you turn purpose and vision into daily action.

Communities with a strong sense of purpose and bold vision will burn out without clearly defined values. Grand ideas aren't enough to sustain individual contributors. Only values can do that, because values are what we interact with every day.

If Harley-Davidson were just a motorcycle company, they would only attract hardcore riders. But Harley is also beloved by soccer moms, retirees, and students who just ride on the weekends. They even have fans who don't ride motorcycles at all. Why? Because people from all walks of life are attracted to their core values of freedom, heritage, community, and quality.

Another example of values in action is GitLab's open-source philosophy, which serves as a code of conduct for its volunteers. Open source is a core value that their community depends upon. If GitLab reversed its position on open-source contributions, it would destroy their ecosystem. Open source as a core value attracts many people, but also repels people who prefer order and control. Open source isn't always easy, but for GitLab, it's the right way.

Startup Grind's values helped to guide not just the grand vision of the community, but also the everyday interactions between members. Every Startup Grind event gives ample time for members to mingle and make friends. SG chapter leaders work hard to connect members to funding and business opportunities. They limit self-promotion at meetups to promote their value of helping others before helping yourself. These values guide Startup Grind's leadership team as well. Like many startup communities, Startup Grind has the network and access to funding to start its own investment vehicle. Instead, they created the Startup Membership, an invite-only community that gives startups free access to fund-raising opportunities, networking, mentorship, and education. They're living their values by serving as the connector between startups, money, and talent.

What does it look like when there's misalignment between members, employees, and a community's values? Unfortunately I have firsthand experience here.

I once had a boss who would set 5:00 p.m. meetings that would drag late into the evening. Sometimes, we wouldn't get out of work until 8:00 or 9:00 p.m. My boss was unmarried with no children. He was a worka-holic, and he wanted his employees to be workaholics too. Our values were not aligned. Working all the time nearly destroyed my family life. I exited the company as quickly as I could, and I will never make that mistake again.

It's your turn. What are your values? I'm sure you can name a few off the top of your head.

Questions for Defining Your Values:

+ How would your closest colleagues describe you?
+ When building this community, what is nonnegotiable for you?

- What do you do every day?
- Example: Start conversations in community, exercise, meet someone new, create something
- Is there a version of your community you wouldn't want to be a part of? What does it look like?

WHEN MOTIVATION RUNS DRY, REMEMBER YOUR WHY.

Company and community leaders will change every few years or so. What stays consistent is your Why.

Creating a powerful Why doesn't just accelerate growth and build your brand—it's the secret behind turning customers into raving fans. Once you have a clear idea of your purpose, vision, and values, move onto the next rule, where we'll discuss the magic of big goals.

RULE 4:

SET AN
INSPIRING GOAL

"START WITH
DEFINING THE
COURAGEOUS."

THE VERY FIRST Traction Conf—held in that dark, grimy concert hall in downtown Vancouver—almost never happened at all.

Despite the popularity of our meetups, making the leap from pizzas to keynotes was no joke. Calculating the total cost of gifts for speakers and volunteers, venue fees, event production, food, security, and other expenses, the first Traction Conf came out to over $250,000.

Our budget? Zilch. Goose egg. We had nothing in the bank to fund a conference.

If you're unfamiliar with the economics of conferences, it typically works like this: You always plan to lose money on your first conference. Your only goal should be to build your brand. Then you try to break even on your second conference, and finally turn a profit on your third.

For us, though, we didn't have cash to burn on that first conference. Traction would have to be profitable from the jump. Could we do it? As the old Henry Ford saying goes, whether you think you can or think you can't, you're right.

I took the lead on sales. The goal was ambitious but clear: we'd need to sell five hundred tickets to break even, and we had just three months to do it. I started by breaking down the goal into a series of steps and experiments. First, we loaded our website with social proof—testimonials from influential speakers and logos of the companies they represented. Then we looked for the most effective marketing channels. To sell five hundred tickets, we'd have to reach a *lot* of people. Traction's audience wasn't big enough yet, but what if we could tap into the audiences of our speakers? They had a combined ten *million* followers. I made it dead simple for them to share the event on social media and asked (ok, begged) them to help. Many of them did, and for that I'm eternally grateful. We also tapped into our community partners—a network of startup incubators, accelerators, and influential founders. They were absolute rockstars who further increased our social proof and reach. Some experiments didn't pan out, like running paid social ads (we had one ad variation that performed modestly, but this was by far our weakest channel.) I'll spare you the rest of the details for now. You can get my exact playbook for marketing and promoting this conference by downloading our bonus content at www.lloyedlobo.com/bonus.

By the end of the first weekend, we sold $50,000 worth of pre-sale tickets. Early bird tickets were gone in one week. And with a full forty-five days before the event, we had reached capacity. In the end, the first Traction Conf reached over $250,000 in revenue and turned a modest profit. We donated the proceeds to Launch Academy, a nonprofit startup incubator.

Having a strong Why is critical for building a long-term, sustainable community. But one thing your Why can't provide is *urgency*.

"Acting with speed will garner you respect, awe, and irresistible momentum," says Robert Greene in his book, *The 33 Strategies of War*. Speed and urgency will help you build momentum and attract the very best to your cause.

The most powerful source of urgency is a big, hairy, inspiring goal.

THE POWER OF INSPIRATIONAL GOALS

I've always believed that big goals pull you forward. They inspire you to reach heights you never imagined. Case in point: Noah Kagan.

After finishing his tenure as employee number thirty at Facebook, Noah Kagan took a job as head of marketing for a stealth startup called Mint.com. Mint's big Why was to simplify personal finance for everyday people. But this was 2006 and Mint had a lot of competition. So founder Aaron Patzer gave Kagan not just an inspirational goal, but a seemingly impossible one: sign up 100,000 Mint.com users in six months.

Unrattled by the enormous mission, Kagan got to work with urgency. First he worked backward from his target goal to create a daily execution plan for the next six months (this plan became known simply as the Mint Marketing Plan). Kagan and his team worked feverishly to grow Mint's user base, testing dozens of growth channels and then doubling down on what worked best. At the end of six months, how many users do you think Mint had? Not 100,000. Not 150,000. In just 180 days, Mint.com attracted over one *million* new users.

That's the power of an inspirational goal. Less than two years later, Mint.com sold to Intuit for over $170 million. The startup's most valuable asset? Their large and engaged user base.

But what if your goal isn't to be as big as possible? What if you choose to define success differently?

You can still use the power of big, inspirational goals to generate urgency.

Take HubSpot, an all-in-one sales, marketing, and customer service platform. Today, HubSpot is a SaaS giant—a publicly traded company worth almost $20 billion. But back in the mid 2000s, it was just another upstart marketing platform. Kipp Bodnar, HubSpot's current CMO, started at the company in 2010 as an inbound marketing strategist. His job was to help HubSpot become *the leader* in the insanely competitive MarTech space.

Like Kagan, Bodnar's goal was massive, but he took a slightly different approach to addressing it. Instead of focusing on the sheer number of new HubSpot users, Bodnar challenged his team with a single, inspiring question: "How do we win the 'marketing internet' this week?"

Success comes down to doing just one or two things really well, repeatedly over time. Bodnar's question generated massive urgency each and every week. His team responded with the most creative content in the industry. They focused on understanding the marketing community better than anyone. Not only did they win the marketing internet most weeks, they created raving fans (and dozens of imitators) in the process.

But it's not always about what you do. Sometimes, it's about who you serve.

Remember Joseph Quan's vision for CPOHQ? He wanted to build the premier community for HR executives. To achieve this vision, he set a goal for his team to attract 1,000 CPOs and Heads of HR. This may not seem like a massive goal, but think of the audience. CPOs are some of the busiest executives in the world, and there are still very few of them. Landing just a single member is a huge undertaking and a massive win. Quan was going after whales, not minnows. The story of *Moby Dick* reminds us just how inspiring and all-consuming whale hunting can be.

Inspiring goals come in many shapes and sizes. It doesn't need to be a huge number to motivate you and your team.

SETTING THE RIGHT GOAL

But big, inspiring goals are useless—even harmful—if they're the *wrong* goals. And unfortunately, there are many ways to set the wrong goal.

We've been told to set goals since we were little kids. But no one ever taught us *how* to set goals. We typically pick a big number that sounds good and impresses people. But we soon realize that a) it's not attainable, b) it's not useful, or c) we don't even know what the goal is.

To set the *right* goals for your community, start by asking yourself three questions:

QUESTION 1: IS IT COURAGEOUS AND QUANTIFIABLE?

What makes a goal truly inspiring? There are two key characteristics.

First, it must be courageous. Your goal should be in service of your higher purpose, but it should also scare you a bit. Most people wouldn't dare take on such a massive goal, but *your* community does! An inspiring goal requires every ounce of your collective energy and focus to achieve. Yet it's not so big that it feels impossible (more on this in Question 2).

Second, your goal needs to be quantifiable with a scoreboard and a deadline. Otherwise, you'll never know if you really achieved the goal or not.

Mint.com's goal of 100,000 users in six months was clearly quantifiable and courageous. (In hindsight, though, what would have happened if founder Aaron Patzer had set his sights on 500,000 users, or even one million? Knowing Kagan, he would have blown that goal out of the park as well.)

Kipp Bodnar's goal for HubSpot was also courageous and quantifiable. It takes guts to declare you will *win the internet* (even just a sliver of it). And by tracking website visitors and mentions on forums like Reddit, the HubSpot team could clearly see whether or not they succeeded each week.

CPOHQ's goal was clearly courageous. Approaching C-suite executives and asking them to join your online community is bold. But Quan's goal was also quantifiable. He created a clear scoreboard for his team: attract the top HR executive from 1,000 major companies. Each new community member was another point on the board.

In 2020, Kagan came on the *Traction Podcast* and pushed me to set a courageous and quantifiable goal:

Grow the Traction email list from 30,000 subscribers to over 100,000 by the end of the year. Our trajectory at that point was under 50,000 for the year. Using many of the strategies in the Mint Marketing Plan, we reached 96,000 subscribers by January.

This story illustrates another lesson: even if you miss your big, inspirational goal, you'll wind up miles ahead of where you thought you could be.

As you think about setting your own inspiring goal, start with defining the courageous. What goal would you be absolutely thrilled to reach? Now double that. How do you feel now? If your goal doesn't make you a little nervous, you're not thinking big enough. Quan didn't say he wanted to build *one of* the premier communities for HR people: he wanted to be *the* premier community. The best. Don't sell yourself short.

Once you've defined the courageous, it's time to build your scoreboard. How will you measure your success? Is it by new sign ups, social media traffic, comments on your community forum, or something else? Whatever your metric, make sure you and your team can see it constantly. Pin it at the top of your online dashboard. Create a separate channel in your chat tool to give updates. We'll talk in detail about choosing the right metrics in Rule 13: Measure and Monetize.

Lastly, make your goal time bound. Patzer gave Kagan six months to hit his goal of 100,000 users. Bodnar gave his team seven days to win the marketing internet, and the clock reset each week. For the first Traction Conf, we had just three months to build a profitable event.

Set a deadline for yourself, then cut it by 33 percent. This will generate the type of urgency that will push you past your false limitations.

This first question is where most people stop when setting their goals, but the next two are absolutely critical for setting the *right* goals.

QUESTION 2: IS IT ATTAINABLE?

When Kagan set out on his goal to land 100,000 new Mint.com users in six months, he didn't start sending emails and posting on social media right away. He made a plan. His plan (the Mint Marketing Plan) started with the courageous, quantifiable, and inspiring goal at the top of the page. Then he worked *backward*, step-by-step, to make sure it was attainable.

Kagan created a spreadsheet of every possible new growth channel: *TechCrunch*, Reddit, Google Search, Google Ads, his personal website, and many more. Then he figured out the approximate reach of each channel (i.e., how much daily traffic they received). Finally, he estimated the click through rate (CTR) and conversion rate of each channel. This gave Kagan an estimated number of new users he could expect from each channel. For example, if a *Tech-Crunch* article about Mint.com could get 300,000 views, with a 10 percent CTR and 25 percent conversion rate, Kagan could expect 7,500 new users from that channel.

He scrutinized every channel and added up the potential users until the total number reached 100,000. The better he understood a channel, the higher his confidence in his projections.

Eisenhower said that plans are useless, but planning is essential. Was Kagan 100 percent accurate in his growth projections? Absolutely not. But his research gave him confidence that his goal was attainable.

QUESTION 3: IS IT ALIGNED WITH YOUR BUSINESS GOALS?

No community lives in a vacuum. Even nonprofit communities need funding to survive. Ask yourself, is your community goal aligned with your business needs?

Kagan's goal of 100,000 new users was directly aligned with Mint.com's business goals. But goal alignment is not always this obvious. For example, why did Bodnar of HubSpot set the goal to "win the marketing internet each week" instead of acquiring new users? The answer can be found in HubSpot's larger vision: to change the way companies grow by introducing a new paradigm called *inbound marketing*. Before HubSpot, technology companies relied on sales, advertising, and outbound marketing tactics like direct mail. These channels are expensive and time-consuming. Inbound marketing is all about *attracting* new customers instead of chasing them. The success of inbound marketing is predicated on getting your target customer's attention. This is what drove the goal to win the marketing internet each week.

Why did Joseph Quan set out to build the premier community for Heads of HR? Why not build the *largest* community of HR professionals instead? It's because Quan's company, Knoetic, provides HR analytics and benchmarks that CPOs need to do their jobs. Every CPOHQ member is a potential Knoetic customer. The community and the business are perfectly aligned.

Let's talk about that first Traction Conf again. Why was it so important to run a profitable event? Simply put, we did not have a marketing budget. As a bootstrapped company, we couldn't afford to lose hundreds of thousands of dollars on a conference. It had to pay for itself or we'd go belly up.

To ensure your community goals are aligned with your company goals, ask yourself:

1. What will be the impact on our business if we hit our community goal?
2. What *won't* happen within our business if we hit our community goal?

Make sure your community success and business success are pointing in the same direction.

GOAL EVALUATION TOOL: THE RICE FRAMEWORK

The three questions we just discussed are a great place to start evaluating your big, hairy, inspiring goals.

Now take it a step further by using the RICE Framework, a prioritization tool developed by the customer service platform, Intercom.

RICE stands for *Reach, Impact, Confidence, and Effort*—it's a powerful framework to help you decide which tactics and channels to try first.

Reach is the number of target customers who will come into contact with your company through an event, campaign, or community. For example, all 110,000 Traction community members came in contact with Boast. AI through every email, webinar, and event we ran. But reach also means connecting with the *right* people. If your community members don't spend a lot of time on Instagram, don't use Instagram. Go where your people are.

Impact represents the level of transformation your community goal will have on your business. By winning the marketing internet each week, HubSpot saw dramatic user growth with each viral piece of content. Again, ask the two questions I shared in the previous section:

1. What will be the impact on our business if we hit our community goal?
2. What *won't* happen within our business if we hit our community goal?

Confidence refers to your level of knowledge of a particular channel or tactic. The better you understand a channel, the more confident you can be in your projections. If you're planning to experiment with a brand-new channel, expect a higher degree of variance in the outcome. This is important to consider when prioritizing your limited time and resources.

Finally, *Effort* represents the time and resources you must commit to your campaign. Large events like Traction Conf are high effort, so our confidence in its success needs to be just as high. However, our small pizza nights were low effort both in terms of money and time spent.

When you're just starting out, don't commit to high-effort activities until you're confident it will have the impact on your business you expect. Think big, but start small.

RICE FRAMEWORK

CHANNEL	REACH	IMPACT	CONFIDENCE	EFFORT	RICE SCORE
COMMUNITY	450	3	100%	2	675
SDR	2,000	1	80%	4	400
SEO	1,000	2	50%	3	333

RICE SCORE = (REACH X IMPACT X CONFIDENCE) ÷ EFFORT
Source: Sean McBride, Intercom

Big, inspiring goals are highly motivating. You'll be ready to strap on rocket boosters and blast your community into orbit.

But before you start to build, you need to find your people. That's next.

RULE 5:

FIND YOUR PEOPLE

"YOUR IDEAL MEMBERS ARE ALREADY HANGING OUT TOGETHER."

N 2004, my girlfriend Viveta (who I was lucky enough to marry in 2009), told me about a new website that had just launched at her university, Rutgers. It was called The Facebook. I was at Lakehead University at the time, and The Facebook's campus-by-campus expansion plan kept me locked out. FOMO wasn't a phrase back then, but I absolutely had it.

When The Facebook first launched in February 2004, it was only available to Harvard University students. Within the first month, half of Harvard's undergraduates had signed up. It then expanded to other elite schools like Yale, Columbia, Stanford, and Dartmouth. By fall it was available at other universities like Rutgers. By the end of 2004, anyone with a .edu email address could join, which is when I hopped on the speeding train. It wasn't until September 2006—two and a half years after its launch—that The Facebook (by then just called Facebook) opened its network to anyone over the age of thirteen.

It was clear Mark Zuckerberg and his co-founders were sitting on a rocket ship. Why did they constrain their growth? It took Facebook four years and six months to reach 100 million users. Could they have reached that number in three years? Two? It's possible. But I believe it would have killed the company and its burgeoning community.

The first version of Facebook was nothing like it is today. There was no marketplace, no groups, no events, and no open graph newsfeed, which today is the center of the Facebook experience. The only features were profile pages, pictures, and a cheeky little feature called Relationship Status. This was where The Facebook users shared whether they were single, in a relationship, or the most titillating, "It's Complicated."

It was the Relationship Status that made The Facebook spread like wildfire. As a social media platform for college students, nothing was more important than the irresistible intrigue of the campus dating life: who was pairing up, who was newly single, and where to take your shot. This single piece of information dictated which classes you signed up for next semester (to be with that newly single love interest) and your plans for the weekend. It was The Facebook's killer feature—the Why behind its early community.

Did Zuckerberg have bigger goals than to build a dating site for college students? Of course. The clarity of his long-term vision is startup lore. It's why he dropped out of Harvard and moved out to Silicon Valley. But before all that, Zuckerberg had the patience to find and focus on his people: his college classmates.

Now imagine if Facebook had invited anyone to sign up in its early days: parents, professionals, creeps who wanted to spy on college students, and even the authorities. In this imaginary version of Facebook, how many college students would have been willing to post something as personal as their relationship status? How many would post photos of themselves out with their friends, partying and having a good time? Plus, how many different features would Facebook have been compelled to build for their varied audience? Parents and mid-career professionals care far less about relationship status.

Would they have asked for features to track their children? Job boards to find their next gig? Professional networking groups? All of these things now exist on Facebook, but at the time, it would have watered down the experience to the point of irrelevance.

The biggest loss for this imaginary version of Facebook is *network effects*. Had Facebook been open to everyone right away, users would've been more likely to encounter strangers on the platform than friends. Previous social networks—like MySpace and Friendster—operated this way. They thought people wanted to make *new* friends online. In a stroke of genius, Zuckerberg flipped the script: he connected real-life friends on the internet. Facebook's campus-by-campus rollout ensured every new user already knew people on the network. Everyone had to sign up with their real identities, making it easier to find friends and mutual connections. This led to greater trust in the platform, more rapid word-of-mouth expansion, and eventually, social media dominance.

Facebook's decision to limit growth was the best thing they could have done. It's a masterclass in building community: to succeed early on, you must find your people and serve them exceptionally well.

THE VALUE OF FOCUS

Community builders are ambitious folks. You have to be driven (and a little hardheaded) to believe you can rally people around a strong Why and deliver on a massive vision. But we tend to fixate on one word that can lead us astray: *growth*. Whether your goal is an exclusive club of the 1,000 top leaders in your industry (like CPOHQ), or millions of members in chapters around the globe (Harley-Davidson), you're probably focused on getting there as fast as possible.

For many communities, the most dangerous obstacle is impatience. We've all seen groups that try too hard to grow and lose the magic that made them special in the first place. They seem to suffer from a chronic lack of focus, throwing mud against the wall to see what sticks. This often leads to the opposite effect: slower growth, higher churn, and a steady decline in overall membership.

Don't hear what I'm not saying; impatience is a valuable trait for a founder and community builder. The previous rule was all about generating urgency. Set a big, inspiring goal and go for it. But don't become so impatient that you lose sight of your most important asset: your people.

When you find and focus on one group of people—instead of two, five, or even a dozen (I've seen this firsthand)—you're able to do things that don't scale. You can create a community experience that feels handcrafted and personalized, because it is. When your entire community has common interests, needs, and goals (e.g., finding a love interest), you can then create killer community experiences that keep them coming back for more (e.g., relationship status).

This is the path Sales Hacker took when building their community for sales professionals. "We started with a high-quality group of really happy customers," co-founder Max Altschuler told me on a Traction live webinar, "We started with ten to twenty people and made sure they were getting a ton of value. We stayed in that range [of members] for three to six months."

Would you have the patience to stay that small for a quarter or more? Many community builders don't, and the cost is greater than any growth generated in the early days. When you focus on your people, you get to learn from your mistakes without destroying your reputation.

"Those ten to twenty [early members] were very forgiving," Altschuler said. "When you grow too fast and you don't know what levers to pull . . . you end up in this no-man's-land. You have a bunch of people in this thing, they aren't really engaging with each other, and you don't know what metrics to track. Eventually members leave, and any little spark of community you hoped to ignite goes out for good."

If done right, your early community members don't just become your biggest fans; they teach you what type of community you need to build. This was the real secret behind Facebook's ascent. "The brilliance of Mark Zuckerberg was his willingness to allow Facebook to go wherever the market wanted it," said *Forbes* contributor Adam Hartung back in 2011.

Zuck didn't force growth, nor did he build features the community didn't ask for. Facebook experimented daily, listened to feedback, and focused relentlessly on its core users.

Your early members are critical to the long-term success of your community. But how do you find the right people to seed your upstart group?

FIND YOUR ICP: IDEAL COMMUNITY PERSONA

I think of building community in the same way as building a product. The most important question to answer in the early days is this: Who are we serving?

In other words, we're looking for your ICP: your ideal *community* persona.

You may be familiar with the other ICP: the ideal customer persona. Companies use this ICP to build a picture of their target customer. It often includes demographic information like job, location, and income, as well as psychographic traits like their goals, challenges, and values. This is a good model for community builders. From here on out, when I say ICP, I'll be referring to the ideal *community* persona.

Having a clear ICP will help you seed your community with people who share your purpose, vision, and values—your Why. It will also help you repel or weed out bad-fit members. Your early members will attract like-minded people, so be sure you want more of those people.

It's time to create a picture of ICP—your people. We can do this with just six questions:

1. Who do you want to serve?
2. What are their key jobs?
3. What are their secondary jobs?
4. What does their delighted state look like?
5. What stands in their way?
6. What are their three Fs?

Let's dig into each question.

QUESTION 1: WHO DO YOU WANT TO SERVE?

Leaders exist to help the community, not the other way around. So a great place to start in finding your people is this: who do you want to serve?

Max Altschuler wanted to serve his fellow B2B salespeople. He wanted to make their lives easier and their careers more fruitful. Altschuler built the community he wished he had when he got into sales.

For me, I have always aimed to serve tech entrepreneurs. I firmly believe that startups can change the world. I've seen firsthand how they can make people's lives better. Through Traction, we contributed to building a thriving startup scene in Vancouver alongside many others in the ecosystem. The scope of our events has grown, but our focus on tech entrepreneurs has always been the same.

When deciding who you want to serve, be as specific as possible. Don't just say, "I want to serve restaurant owners." Instead, define what type of restaurant owner you want to serve, the challenges they face, and the future you want to help them build. For example, "I want to serve immigrant restaurant owners who are trying to acclimate to life in America and want to build businesses they can pass down to their children." The more vivid your description, the easier it will be to find and serve your ideal community members.

If you're struggling to identify a community you wish to serve, don't worry. It doesn't make you a bad or selfish person. In fact, it might mean you're so close to the group, you're failing to recognize it. When in doubt, aim to *scratch your own itch*, as they say.

What community would *you* want to be part of? Like Altschuler with Sales Hacker and me with Traction, build a community you wish you could be part of. Chances are you aren't the only one looking for it.

QUESTION 2: WHAT ARE THEIR KEY JOBS?

Every person has *jobs* they need to perform to be successful. I'm not talking about a literal *j-o-b*, like an engineer or restaurant owner, but a set of primary responsibilities that must be done. For B2B salespeople in the Sales

Hacker's community, one of their key *jobs* is building and maintaining relationships with potential customers. Another is refining their pitch and persuasion skills. As a restaurant owner, some of your key jobs include hiring staff, sourcing products, cutting costs, and marketing to your local community.

Your ICP's key jobs will serve as the pillars of your community experience. For communities of practice, key jobs include growth and mastery of a skillset. Sales Hacker, HubSpot, and Duolingo are all examples. Communities of play exist to help members fulfill non-work-related jobs. For Harley-Davidson HOG members, it's the job of escaping the real world and feeling free. For Red Bull, it's the job of living life to the fullest. Communities of product help members master a certain tool or platform.

But no matter the type of community, one of *your* key jobs is to help members build connections and relationships. Otherwise, your members might as well read a textbook.

QUESTION 3: WHAT ARE THEIR SECONDARY JOBS?

If you really want to blow away your early members, help them complete their secondary jobs as well. Secondary jobs are the little things that support their key jobs. For example, salespeople need to write emails and maintain their CRM. Harley riders need to insure their bikes. Entrepreneurs need to systematize HR, finance, and project management logistics.

Secondary jobs can steal precious time from us. Strive to create content, products, and resources that help your members get their time back. Sales Hacker, for example, has built a library of templates for members to quickly draft sales emails, qualify leads, track sales activity, and much more. Atlassian's community knowledge base uses a tagging system to ensure members can quickly surface the content they need to answer any question. Harley-Davidson's HOG members get discounts on things like motorcycle insurance and maintenance. A small but underrated job that Facebook solves? Helping users remember birthdays.

Prioritize solving key jobs for your members. Then go above and beyond by solving the secondary jobs as well.

QUESTION 4: WHAT DOES THEIR DELIGHTED STATE LOOK LIKE?

Imagine if you helped your members complete all their jobs in a breeze and knocked down all their barriers. What would their lives look like? Would they have more money, more free time, more opportunities, or all of the above? In what new ways would they go out and change the world?

Paint a vivid picture of this delighted state. For Harley-Davidson, the delighted state looks like a rider on her motorcycle, driving down the open road, wind whipping in her hair, with a pack of friends riding by her side. She's happy and free. The HOG communities are designed to get more members to experience this delighted state by organizing rides and, of course, getting members on the latest and greatest bikes.

For Atlassian community members, the delighted state looks like every team member on the same page. It looks like every piece of information in the right place, available to whomever needs it, and communication flowing smoothly. It looks like a color-coded Gantt chart with an "Ahead of schedule" project status.

So what's stopping your members from reaching this delighted state?

QUESTION 5: WHAT STANDS IN THEIR WAY?

Answering this question is how you turn tentative new members into raving fans. The most beloved communities help members to fulfill their jobs, including the "job" of connecting with others. They provide content and resources, events and opportunities, friendships, and partnerships. If you can identify the obstacles that stand in their way, you will win the day.

Sales Hacker knows all too well the obstacles that B2B salespeople face. This is partly because Max Altschuler is a former B2B salesperson, but also because he spent so much time with his early members. He knows the challenge of crafting the perfect cold email. He knows winning over the personal assistant of an executive is crucial to making the big sale. He knows a lack of feedback can stunt someone's career. Sales Hacker addresses these obstacles and many more with content and connections.

For startup founders, the list of obstacles can feel endless, but a massive one is traction. Gaining customers solves a lot of problems, including the challenges of attracting investment and talent. We use the Traction community to connect startup founders to experts who've achieved breakthrough growth.

QUESTION 6: WHAT ARE THEIR THREE FS?

Your ideal members are already hanging out together. Many of them already work together, go to conferences together, follow the same thought leaders, and use the same products and services. By tapping into their existing networks, your community will feel like a natural extension of their lives. Map out this existing network using the 3 F's framework from entrepreneur and startup coach, Dan Martell:

1. Who do your members *Fund*?
2. Who do they *Follow*?
3. Where do they *Frequent*?

Inspired by Dan Martell's 3 F's Framework

THE FIRST F—fund—refers to the tools, products, and services your ideal members pay for. This is an excellent source of new members because they already have so much in common: jobs to be done and current solutions to that problem. Plus, they might have shared training needs for certain tools. These companies are also potential partners for your community. Zendesk was a platinum sponsor of Traction Conf because we had so many community members and customers in common.

THE SECOND F—follow—refers to the influencers and stars in your industry. In the early days of Sales

Hacker, Altschuler was able to land Daniel Pink on his podcast, which created a wave of new interest in the community. Build relationships with the influencers in your industry. Their followers will become your followers.

THE LAST F—frequent—is all about going where your ideal members already hang out. When Red Bull began building its community in the late 1980s, it didn't immediately set out to create its own events. They sponsored athletes on the world's largest stages, including Formula One racing and the Olympics. Red Bull still follows this strategy today. They don't just try to attract eyeballs; they go where the eyeballs are.

In the early days, it's usually easier to grow on platforms your members already frequent, like Facebook or Discord. As you grow, you can migrate to an owned channel built with a community-specific tool like Mighty Networks. You could also monetize your existing WhatsApp, Telegram, or Discord community using a tool like Nas.io.

PUTTING IT ALL TOGETHER: CREATE YOUR ICP PROFILE

Imagine one of those old-timey *Wanted* posters you see in American Western films. They have a picture of a bad guy at the top, followed by their name, defining features, and alleged crimes. The sheriff hangs up this poster in the center of town so everyone knows to look out for them.

After you answer these six questions in detail, your job is to create a *Wanted* poster for your ideal community member—your ICP profile.

Your ICP profile is a list of traits, jobs, obstacles, and influences that you'll use to attract and screen early members. It's a one-page document that includes a photo, name, and answers to the second set of questions in this section:

1. Who do you want to serve? (Include specific career, job title, or hobby)
2. What are their key jobs?
3. What are their secondary jobs?
4. What does their delighted state look like?
5. What stands in their way?
6. What are their three Fs? (Who do they fund, follow, and frequent?)

The best ICP profiles are based on *actual* people. Identify an early community member that you'd love to clone 10,000 times (i.e., someone you'd be absolutely thrilled to have in your community). Use their actual name, photo, job title, and goals. If possible, ask them these questions directly and record their answers verbatim. You can then use their own words to attract like-minded members.

You may already have a clear idea of who you're trying to attract to your community. Maybe you're still trying to figure it out. Either way, having an ICP will help you focus on finding your people and delivering an exceptional experience.

Once you find your people, it's time to nail the community experience.

RULE 6:

NAIL THEN SCALE

"CREATING AN EXCEPTIONAL COMMUNITY EXPERIENCE STARTS WITH CONNECTING WITH MEMBERS ONE-ON-ONE."

I WAS STANDING IN the Dr. Sun Yat Sen Classical Chinese Garden in Vancouver, British Columbia, admiring the palette of brightly colored leaves and immaculately manicured garden beds. As I took in the scene, the former CEO of Intercom approached me and struck up a conversation. She wanted to talk about the food on her plate. It was *surprisingly* delicious. Not just the best conference food she's had, but some of the best, period.

I'm glad she was surprised and delighted by the meal. I was certainly delighted but far from surprised. This was the 2019 Traction Conf Opening Ceremony. We tried to go above and beyond in every detail for our conference members. If these founders were going to take time out of their insanely busy schedules to attend our conference, we were going to treat them right.

The circular garden was filled with flowers, shrubs, small Japanese maples, and black bamboo. Paths were cut through the center to give visitors a short-but-serene nature walk. The air was a fragrant mix of blossoms and gourmet finger foods. The DJ played music from the elevated Chinese pavilion in the center of the garden. Food stations were set up around the perimeter of the garden, allowing attendees to travel, eat, and bump into old friends as well as new acquaintances. The Zen-like tranquility eased the minds of even the most high-strung executives. The group seemed to enter a collective flow state as we talked, laughed, and made lifelong memories.

Traction is known as the startup conference that nails the little details, but we weren't always this polished (need I remind you of setting the stage on fire?) It took time to get it right.

In the early days of building your community, you'll find yourself doing a lot of manual tasks that big communities would never do. It's a lot of work, but it's also your competitive advantage. This is your one chance to handcraft an exceptional, mind-blowing, tell-everyone-you-know type experience for your early members.

During the pizza party days of Traction, Alex and I personally invited every person who attended. When they arrived, we greeted each one personally and got to know them. We introduced them to others in the room with similar interests and backgrounds. We were the connective tissue for early members. Eventually, our members started inviting their own friends, and soon the events became too big for us to talk to each person individually. But through these early conversations, we got to know our people on an intimate level and craft an experience just for them.

Max Altschuler did the same thing in the early days of Sales Hacker. He had one-on-one conversations with each member to understand their jobs, goals, challenges, and what success looked like to them. "Those early users gave us feedback on each iteration of the Sales Hacker community," he told me.

Harley-Davidson's leadership team handcrafted the HOG experience for *five years* before its official launch. Starting in 1978, the company organized a series of cross-country rides with customers and members of the management team. "We saw it as a way to get out on the road, reconnect with customers, and have some fun," said Willie G. Davidson, grandson of the co-founder and author of *100 Years of Harley-Davidson*. When HOG officially launched in 1983, it already had 30,000 members across the country.

The pattern here is clear: creating an exceptional community experience starts with connecting with members one-on-one. In fact, the best communities never stop this practice. If you search Atlassian's community forum, you won't find a single post without a comment on it within the first hour. The majority of these comments are written by volunteer community leaders.

"Once you understand what your community needs," said Max Altschuler, "then you can start to grow it outside of those numbers."

Don't force your community to grow. Focus on deeply understanding your ideal members and nailing the community experience. When growth starts to feel inevitable—like a balloon ready to pop, or the momentum of a runaway train—*then* it's time to scale.

BUILDING SUSTAINABLE GROWTH: THE NAIL-THEN-SCALE FRAMEWORK

If you approach building a community in the right order (first, nail the customer experience, *then* scale it) growth doesn't just become easier, it becomes more cost effective. Because when you nail the community experience, your members become your best marketing channel. And that's the best way to grow.

Building Traction gave me firsthand experience in nailing the community experience. But I've also learned from other master community builders like Jason Lemkin of SaaStr, Kipp Bodnar of HubSpot, and dozens of others. Every great community follows a variation of these four stages before truly reaching scale:

1. Validate
2. Community-Market Fit
3. Community-Channel Fit
4. Scale

Let's look at each stage more closely.

STAGE 1: VALIDATE

I believe we're entering the golden age of communities. Thanks to the internet, communication tools like Zoom, and the miracles of modern transportation, it's easier than ever to find your people, no matter what you enjoy or where you live. We are so far from community saturation that it's not even worth thinking about. If you want to build a community around a specific interest of yours, you'll find your people to join you.

But that begs the following questions: What type of community will it be? Why are you starting this community in the first place? What are you aiming to achieve? Who are you serving?

Do these questions sound familiar to you? They should—they are the subjects of each rule prior to this one. What you've done up to this point has been validating your community concept. You're already well on your way through Stage 1. But repetition breeds familiarity, so let's take a step back and talk about how validation fits into the bigger picture.

When building products, validation is the process of confirming there's a problem worth solving and a market who would pay for a solution. Validation for communities is essentially the same.

Community validation is when a few ideal members (your ICPs) agree to join because you've identified a pain point and your Why is resonating. When I sent out emails for the first-ever Traction pizza party, we had about twenty founders RSVP. That's validation.

But don't confuse validation with people supporting you because they like you.

Look for enthusiastic "hell yeah" responses from early members. Do you instantly attract a couple superfans? That's a sign you're on the right track. You'll know your community concept is validated when the *right people* are pounding on the door to join. (Shout out to Derek Sivers for his "hell yeah or no" framework for decision-making.)

If you don't think you've validated your community concept yet, work through Rules 2 through 5 again. Experiment with a different type of community (practice vs. product vs. play), clarify your Why, and adjust your goal to see if you can attract the audience you want to serve. Keep talking to ideal members to learn more about their lives and community needs.

Once you feel confident your community concept has been validated, it's time to create an epic experience. Move on to Stage 2: Community-Market Fit.

STAGE 2: COMMUNITY-MARKET FIT

The term *product-market fit* is so common among startups that it's been rendered meaningless . . . almost.

Product-market fit (PMF) is still useful if you truly understand its meaning. Let's look at its original definition, coined by legendary founder and investor, Marc Andreessen (emphasis mine):

"Product-market fit is being in a **good market** with a product that can **satisfy that market.**"

Product-market fit applies just as much to community building as it does to product development. Is your market (i.e., the pool of potential community members) large enough to meet your business goals? Is your product (i.e., the community experience) something potential members need in their lives? Let's call that *community-market fit* (CMF).

The difference between nailing CMF and not can be subtle. For example, Traction Conf and Startup Weekend essentially serve the same purpose: help innovative founders change the world. But our approaches are quite different. Startup Weekend is an immersive, weekend-long sprint where you build a prototype company in seventy-two hours. Traction Conf is a content-driven community with live and online events.

If we traded programming with Startup Weekend, most of our community would revolt and leave, and vice versa. That's because Startup Weekend appeals to a younger crowd that's curious about startups, while Traction serves established founders and executives looking to drive business growth. We both aim to connect entrepreneurs to mentors, investors, and partners, but Startup Weekend does this through a pitch competition and Traction hosts summits and conferences. Same purpose, unique community experiences.

Community-market fit often takes time to find. How do you know if you're on track? The first sign is that your members will start inviting their friends and colleagues. These early evangelists are your greatest asset. Recognize and reward them for their efforts (more on that in Rule 10).

But you may not have evangelists right away, and that's ok. That means you have work to do.

First, focus on building one-on-one relationships with your audience. Ask them questions to understand their goals, challenges, workflows and life-flows. Workflows are the steps and processes they go through to get a job done in their world. For example, when a B2B salesperson needs to understand changing trends in their industry, where do they go? Who do they talk to? What do they read? Life-flows are similar: When busy parents want to hang out with friends, what are their go-to activities? Do they join a social volleyball league? Attend a group dinner? Play video games online?

Next, manufacture connections between members. One of my favorite examples of this is from Sales Hacker. In the early days, Altschuler would personally comment on every thread posted on the community forum. He would tag other community members in the post to spark a discussion. Altschuler also tracked engagement on the forum to ensure every member was getting comments on their post.

Here's the brilliant part of Altschuler's strategy: he didn't care about the *total* number of comments on Sales Hacker that day. "If you have nine threads and fifty comments, but one thread is getting all those comments and the other eight have zero comments, those eight people who wrote those threads are getting zero value," he told me on the *Traction Podcast*.

Instead, Altschuler focused on increasing the *median* number of comments per post. He wanted every contributing member to feel the value of Sales Hacker, not just the lucky few with edgy insights.

Sales Hacker found community-market fit by focusing on their north star metric: the median number of comments per post. You should also have a North Star metric. For many communities, it's Daily Active Users or

Weekly Active Users. For others, it's Net Promoter Score or Brand Affinity score. Another interesting metric comes from Superhuman, the email tool for super connectors. Founder Rahul Vohra steered the company toward product-market fit using a single question he posed to customers every quarter: "How disappointed would you be if Superhuman no longer existed?" When Superhuman first started tracking this metric, only 22 percent of customers said they would be "very disappointed." In just a few years, that number jumped to over 58 percent.

Finding community-market fit is the *nail* in the Nail-Then-Scale framework. It's absolutely essential to get right. This is where patience is critical. Keep hand-crafting the member experience until your North Star metric indicates traction and engagement. Only then should you move on to Stage 3.

STAGE 3: COMMUNITY-CHANNEL FIT

To scale your community, you need to identify your most effective channels for growth. Let's call this Community-Channel Fit.

When Yelp was ready to expand internationally, they faced a serious growth problem. What worked in the United States—organic growth through social media—was not working in other countries, like those in Latin America. Yelp needed a different channel to grow in these new communities.

"You can't take an American playbook, apply it overseas, and expect it to work," said Monica Silvestre, who led Yelp's international expansion and today is Global Head of Community at Canva.

Yelp's international playbook was brilliantly simple. First they hired local community managers in each target city. Then the community managers hosted exclusive events around town. They invited the city's top chefs, restaurateurs, and food influencers, and each guest was only allowed to bring a couple friends. Yelp meetups became *the* go-to foodie events in town . . . if you could score an invite. The buzz around Yelp grew quickly and the app gained a foothold in each new market.

Hosting live events sounds wildly inefficient and unscalable for a company like Yelp. And compared to growing via social media, it was. But again, the point isn't just to scale. You need to *nail* the community experience, *then* scale.

For Traction, our yearly conference is the biggest "product" we produce each year. But our core channels are content and email. We produce multiple webinars, podcast episodes, and YouTube videos each week. Content is our top-of-funnel channel that attracts potential Traction members, and our email list is our middle-of-funnel conversion stage. All of this leads to our final goal: getting people to Traction Conf.

How do you know when you've achieved community-channel fit? At a minimum, you've discovered a growth channel that costs you less than the value of a new member. The gold standard is a 3:1 ratio between lifetime value and customer acquisition cost, also known as the LTV:CAC ratio. If the lifetime value of a new member is $1,500, you should spend $500 or less to acquire them. (The same LTV:CAC ratio still applies if your community is a marketing channel for your business.) If you can get your costs to zero—through free channels like word of mouth—then you've hit the jackpot.

Once you've find community-channel fit, it may feel like you're ready for scale. But there's one more stage to ensure you can handle the growth you're about to experience.

STAGE 4: SCALE

Community-market fit and community-channel fit are the prerequisites to growth. They ensure you have the *right* community experience for your market and a *sustainable* method of acquiring new members.

Now it's time to develop the leadership team and tech infrastructure to scale.

Scale means that seventy-five percent of your efforts go to adding fuel to the fire. You're doubling down on your core community experience and your primary growth channel. Your remaining twenty-five percent is spent trying new things like expanding to new markets, adding new products or experiences, and adding new geographies. Every new experiment starts back at *Stage 1: Validate*, and goes through the nail-then-scale cycle again.

As your community begins to grow, you'll inevitably become overwhelmed with member demands. You can't provide individualized service and still keep your eye on the big picture. Nearly all communities, even those that stay intentionally small, rely on community leaders, managers, and volunteers to handle the growing needs of the group.

When it comes to growing your community management team, I see one crucial mistake more than any other: leaders only outsource the tactical components of running the community. They treat their volunteers and managers like task rabbits, assigning them menial jobs and never giving them decision-making power or creative freedom. This is a recipe for burnout. It will also cause you to miss out on the most powerful benefit of all: your volunteers' creativity, passion, and enthusiasm for the community.

"Great leaders don't just cascade goals," Atlassian's COO, Anu Bharadwaj, told me. "They cascade *purpose*."

Scale is more than just processes and procedures. It's about instilling the community's big Why into your volunteers and managers. They, in turn, pass the Why down to the general membership, connecting everyday activities to the community's purpose, vision, and values. When everyone is on board with the big Why, you can trust them to make the right decisions and take the right actions.

We'll dig into fully activating your members in Rule 9: Collaborate with Your Community.

Tech Infrastructure: Less Is More

Now let's talk about tech. My rule of thumb is *less is more*. Many community leaders—especially the nerds like me who love to build things and try out new tools—will over-engineer their community tech stack. This is the equivalent of an app with too many features. The result is a confusing, muddled user experience that hides the core benefit of the product.

Here's a simple framework to ensure you stay focused on what matters most. This again comes from Rahul Vohra, the founder of Superhuman. When building out the product roadmap, Vohra splits his team's time 50/50. Half their time goes to improving the product's core features (i.e., the things Superhuman customers say they love most). The other half goes toward working on requested features that will attract the next cohort of customers. This approach helps maintain a balance of satisfying your best members while still attracting new ones.

Laura Nestler, the former Head of Community at Duolingo (and, ironically, the Head of Community at Yelp before Monica), has another approach to the challenge of over-building. At Traction Conf 2019, she told our audience, "Optimize only to get to the next level, not ten more levels." Build what you need right now—not what you *think* you'll need a few years from now—because plans will inevitably change. Save yourself the wasted effort by building incrementally.

We'll discuss your tech stack in more detail in Rule 12: Show Up Consistently.

GROWTH IS ALWAYS MESSY.

You're going to break things, make mistakes, and let down community members. It's unavoidable. Remember: your goal is not to be perfect, but to respond the right way and do the right thing for your members. There is almost no mistake that won't be forgiven with a sincere apology and a small token of gratitude. Your members will remember the way you treated them when things went wrong.

To build a healthy, highly engaged, sustainable community that grows organically, focus first on the individual member experience. Then find the most natural and effective channel to reach more members. Finally, build the infrastructure and empower people to manage. A community that scales the right way maintains its sense of purpose and identity. It doesn't allow uncontrolled growth to take over. It doesn't let the individual member get lost in the shuffle.

We've spent the first part of this book looking at community growth at a high level: Your type of community, your big Why, your ideal member, your aspirational goal, and your plan to scale. Now we're going to get tactical. You're going to learn how to create an exceptional community experience from beginning to end, starting with the "Aha" Moment.

RULE 7:

CREATE THE "AHA" MOMENT

"NOT WITH A BANG, BUT WITH A HUG AND A FEW GENUINE WORDS OF ENCOURAGEMENT."

THE SIXTH ANNUAL Traction Conf was slated to start in under an hour.

More than a thousand people funneled through the doors of the JW Marriott Parq Grand Ballroom in Vancouver. Their first stop, like any conference, was the check-in booth. Except this one was . . . different.

As attendees made their way through the sun-soaked lobby of the hotel, they didn't find long lines leading to metal folding tables with Sharpies and name tags. Instead, they came across a row of iPads standing on tall tables. Attendees followed the instructions on the screen: click the *sign in* button, then look into the iPad camera. Moments later, their names flashed across the screen and a small printer on the table pumped out their name tag. The process took less than thirty seconds. On the other side of the kiosks, freshly signed-in guests stopped to talk about what just happened. They were buzzing with excitement. "Welcome to the future," I said as I passed by.

Traction is a community for the most innovative entrepreneurs. We're constantly pushing the envelope of what's possible. That means using technology to improve the conference experience. When a Traction community member, TTT Studios, approached us with their facial recognition check-in tool, Amanda AI, it was too cool to pass up.

#YourFaceIsYourTicket became the first "Aha" Moment of the conference. It was a taste of the cutting-edge ideas to come. It told our members, "If you want to be surrounded by innovators, you're in the right place."

Longtime members are the heart and soul of your community. But every long-term member was once a first-time visitor, and many communities suffer from revolving door syndrome. New folks attend a single event and never come back. Why?

Maybe they're a poor fit. Maybe they don't have time. But more often than not, new members churn because they don't see the value of coming back. People are busier and more distracted than ever. If you can't make that lightbulb in their head go off right away, they won't wait around to see what you have to offer.

THE AHA MOMENT: MAKING AN UNFORGETTABLE FIRST IMPRESSION

Think of the last community you joined that just seemed to click. Maybe it was a professional group, a cohort-based course, or a rec softball league. Try to remember the very first moment that made you say, "Yeah, this is what I was looking for." I bet it's clear as day. *That* is the "Aha" Moment.

I recently joined the Nas Creator Accelerator, a community run by YouTuber Nuseir Yassin. He's best known for creating over 1,000 daily, one-minute videos on YouTube, TikTok, and Instagram. His fans know him as

Nas Daily. Even with 40 million subscribers across platforms, he's still one of the most genuine human beings I've ever met. The goal of the accelerator is to help other creators build their personal media brands. There are some seriously impressive people in this community—folks who already have hundreds of thousands of followers—and it would be easy to be intimidated. Except Nas designed the experience to make everyone feel included and connected.

From the very first virtual meetup, I knew I was in the right place. The song "C'est la vie" by Algerian music superstar Khaled blasted through our speakers—its upbeat melody and insanely catchy hook filling us with joy (if you don't know the song, look it up. Tell me it doesn't get you pumped!). Nas then welcomed us with his iconic energy and enthusiasm. He gave every individual a personalized introduction fit for a rockstar. Then Nas handed the virtual mic over to some of his friends. And when I say friends, I mean other social media superstars, each with millions of followers. Everyone shared a piece of advice and encouraged us to take this program seriously. If we committed to the work, it could change our lives. Not only was I starstruck, I was ready to run through walls.

Then we jumped straight into creating. Nas threw out an idea for a video and we workshopped the script together. At the end, Nas gave us our homework for the week: create eight video scripts. Eight! This would be the moment any unserious creator would tap out. For the rest of us, it was like discovering our Hogwarts—the perfect place to hone our skills and achieve our biggest dreams. The first call was three hours long, but it flew by. It was one of the most engaging and memorable experiences of my life.

An unforgettable "Aha" Moment is one that captures every CAMPER principle in a single experience:

+ Connection: Are people friendly and welcoming?

+ Autonomy: Will I have control over my own destiny?

+ Mastery: Will this community push me to be better and help me reach my goals?

+ Purpose: Do their mission, vision, and values align with my own?

+ Energy: Is the experience engaging and stimulating?

+ Recognition: Do I feel seen and valued?

Nas's Creator Accelerator community nailed each principle on that first call. From the group scriptwriting (mastery) to the personalized introductions and praise (recognition) to even the homework assignments (autonomy), it was a massive lightbulb moment for me. There was no doubt I was in the right place.

Does your "Aha" Moment need to be as big and splashy as Nas's? No! You don't need to be friends with YouTube stars to deliver an exceptional first impression. It's more important that your "Aha" Moment aligns with your community's Why. Sometimes, all it takes is a few words of support and encouragement.

Physician Moms Group (PMG) is a community for mothers who are also working physicians or in medical school to become one. It was founded in 2014 by Dr. Hala Sabry, an emergency medical physician and a super-mom of five—with two sets of twins! Dr. Sabry created the group to connect with and support other physician mothers, each facing a unique set of challenges in their personal and professional lives. Today there are over 120,000 PMG members in over one hundred countries, making it the world's largest community dedicated to physician mothers.

I've had a front-row seat to this incredible community for years. My wife, Dr. Viveta Lobo, is a member. Viveta has always been the rock of our family. She kept us afloat as I bootstrapped Boast.AI, all the while being an incredible mother and equally impressive physician. The PMG community supported her every step of the way.

I asked Viveta to share a few words about her "Aha" Moment as a PMG member:

> My 'Aha' Moment was the first time I posted in the group. I was a relatively new attending physician, and I was having a string of really tough emergency medicine shifts, particularly pediatric patients. Lloyed is very squeamish and so I don't generally talk about my EM shifts with him. I had just gotten home past 2:00 a.m. from another tough shift. The house was quiet. Everyone was asleep but I was too wired from my shift to go to bed. I logged into PMG and posted about the shift and my feelings.

Within the hour, I had a dozen comments from other physicians who could relate and truly encourage me. It was just what I needed, and despite not knowing any of them personally, I felt their sincerity and connection. After that, I was hooked. Now, I actively try to log in a few times a week and offer any help or advice I can. I continue to post on all sorts of topics, some just for laughs, others to get a vote on what to wear to my next office Christmas party or to get a recommendation on vacation spots for a family with three kids under age ten. They never disappoint!

Viveta's story is the perfect reminder: sometimes the most profound moments for your members are the quietest. They happen not with a bang, but with a hug and a few genuine words of encouragement.

DESIGN YOUR "AHA": EXCEEDING EXPECTATIONS EVERY DAY

Building a community is like a long-term relationship: a great first impression may get you a second date, but if you want things to last, you'll need to show up and exceed expectations every day. You should strive to make every community touchpoint an "Aha" Moment for your members.

CAMPER is the perfect tool for helping you design everyday "Aha" Moments in your community. Let's go through each principle and brainstorm ways to go above and beyond for your community:

CONNECTION

People crave meaningful connections, especially in the digital-first world we now live in. Social media companies have led us to believe that more followers means more connection, but the opposite is true. We've sacrificed deep relationships for thousands of shallow acquaintances. How can you help your members connect with each other in a real, meaningful way?

Physician Moms Group is a massive community. To encourage deeper relationships between members, PMG has various subgroups. Viveta joined one of these small groups at an extremely difficult time in our lives and found the connection she needed:

> *In 2018, my second child was born four months premature and spent over one hundred days in the hospital before coming home. At the time, I was overwhelmed with emotions and uncertainty. When I posted about it in PMG, someone recommended a secondary group that formed off PMG called Physician Moms for Preemies. I joined this second group and found my people. All of these*

women had experienced just what I was, and the group existed to support each other.

Over those four months I heavily relied on this group, often scrolling through old posts and reading similar experiences. Updates from members who had already been through similar experiences and now had older children that were thriving were like a lifeline to me. They fueled my hope and helped me persevere each uncertain day in the NICU.

I now continue to give back by encouraging that mom in the NICU, answering questions about my experience, and posting updates about my now four-year-old, thriving toddler.

The smaller the group, the easier it is to build connections. Use subgroups and one-on-one breakouts to help members forge real relationships.

PMG also hosts multiple in-person events every year. Like Traction Conf, this is where the strongest relationships are forged. PMG's retreats and summits create life-long friendships that then make the online community even stronger. If your community is primarily online, consider hosting at least one in-person event every year.

AUTONOMY

Humans need autonomy and control over their lives. That's why the best communities have a strong Why, but allow members the freedom to chase it in their own way. Community programming should feel like a real-life adventure game. As the community leader, you lay out the map, goal, and guidelines—then you let your members craft their own ideal experience.

Nas created autonomy in our Creator Accelerator community by giving us homework each week but leaving the assignments open-ended. He told us to create eight video scripts, but *we* got to choose the topics and styles for each video. Nas gave us direction, not instructions.

Business conferences give their members autonomy by offering multiple content tracks for different members. Music festivals enhance the sense of adventure by hosting multiple concerts and activities at the same time. Programming is important in every community, but don't make it rigid. Build flexibility into your community. Let members get creative with how they engage.

MASTERY

Mastery means different things to different people. For those in the Nas Creator Accelerator, we want to grow our online communities through entertaining and educational content. For PMG members like Viveta, it's not just about becoming a better physician and mother, but being the best version of themselves in every way.

PMG encourages members to share resources and information with each other, including job postings, articles, and advice on topics such as childcare and maternity leave. Conversations cover everything from recommendations of baby products to best vacation locations, marital issues to new job opportunities, and getting in shape and the latest fashion trends. PMG also creates mentorship opportunities by pairing experienced physician mothers with newer members. These relationships are invaluable; they give young doctors a leg up in their careers and longtime mentors an outlet to help the next generation of physician moms.

Mastery can take years to achieve, so don't waste time. Shaan Puri—co-host of the *My First Million* podcast (recently acquired by HubSpot)—runs a cohort-based course called Power Writing. Like Nas's scriptwriting exercise, Puri gives his students a writing assignment within the first few minutes of the first class. This move kickstarts the transformation process; it shifts their mindset from "I *want* to be a writer," to "I *am* a writer." That's a huge psychological win that accelerates their learning and success.

Help your members achieve mastery faster by jumping right into the work.

PURPOSE

One of the unique aspects of the PMG is its commitment to social activism and advocacy. The group has been vocal in its support for policies and initiatives that address the needs of physician mothers, such as paid parental leave and family-friendly work environments. The PMG has also been active in advocating for social justice and healthcare equity, and has partnered with organizations such as Black Lives Matter and Doctors Without Borders to support these efforts.

Whatever you believe, put it on display for your members from the very beginning. This will serve you in two ways: First, it will quickly weed out people who don't share your Why, saving you both time. Second, it will immediately strengthen your relationship with the *right* members.

ENERGY

Singing. Laughter. Movement. Conversation. New members should feel like they're walking into a buzzing community from the very first moment. As a YouTube creator, Nas instinctively knew how to create energy in the Nas Creator Accelerator. Music is one of the best ways to set the right mood, whether you're running a high-paced creator cohort or a soothing yoga retreat. If you're hosting live events (physical or digital), *never* let people walk into a silent room.

For async communities that don't hold live events, you can create energy in conversation threads. One benefit of PMG's worldwide community is that there are always members online, even when Viveta gets home at 2:00 a.m. and wants to talk. If your community is based around forum conversations, be sure every member post receives a quick reply—even if it means responding to each post yourself.

RECOGNITION

There are few things more terrifying than being the new kid. If you've never experienced this (lucky you), let me share:

First, you get dropped off in front of a big building you've never seen before. Walking in, you have no idea where you are. If you happen to stumble your way into the right classroom, the teacher will then say something like, "Class, we have a new student today," and then give you a halfhearted introduction. This only serves to draw attention to your strangeness. You sit by yourself for however long it takes for another loner to feel sorry for you and invite you to their table. The assimilation process begins, but it's an awkward and painful one.

This is how your new members feel when they join your community: nervous, awkward, and different. Except unlike the new kid at school, your new members are free to leave whenever they want. And they will if you don't make them feel included.

Make your new members feel like rockstars. Do what Nas did with his personalized introductions: don't just introduce them—*rave* about them. Make it so your existing members can't *wait* to go up and meet this new person. Instead of feeling nervous, your new members should feel proud, respected, and like they belong. Make them feel at home.

(I'm a huge believer in recognizing your members, so much so that I've dedicated Rule 10 to the subject.)

"AHA" MOMENTS ARE ALSO YOUR MOST POWERFUL MARKETING ASSET.

When you blow someone away with a perfectly designed "Aha" Moment, they will tell everyone about your community. That's why I included my experience with Nas's Creator Accelerator Program in this book. That's why Viveta tells every physician mother she meets about PMG.

Every breakthrough tech product has an "Aha" moment as well. Think back to the first time you used Uber. Signup was simple and the UI was intuitive. With a few clicks, you had a car on the way—and you could *see* it coming on the map. No more hailing cabs or paying the driver directly. For most people, once they tried Uber they never went back.

Like great tech products, incredible community experiences don't happen by accident. Spend time and energy on crafting your "Aha" Moments. It's one of the most important investments you can make.

In the next several rules, we're going to discuss specific ways to design the community experience that builds on your "Aha" Moment to keep members continuously interested and active.

First up: engaging multiple senses to delight.

RULE 8:

DESIGN UNFORGETTABLE EXPERIENCES

"ONE THAT DELIGHTS ALL THE SENSES AND BONDS YOU TO THE PEOPLE AROUND YOU."

SAND WAS HITTING my face at a thousand granules per second.

The roar of the silver Toyota Land Cruiser was all I could hear as massive clouds of dust stirred behind us. As we rode up and down the treacherous dunes of the Arabian Desert, our vehicle tilted sideways at angles that seemed to defy gravity. We reached the top of one dune and could see thousands more peaks just like it, surrounding us like a choppy ocean of sand. My kids were in the backseat screaming their heads off—was it out of terror or enjoyment? My wife was sitting next to me, screaming as hard as they were. I'll admit, I was screaming even louder!

Our vacation to Dubai was the highlight of my year—and a much-needed getaway. After a bout with COVID-19 that nearly took my life in 2021, I wanted to spend much more quality time with my family. We decided to get out of our time zone so we could spend uninterrupted time together.

The dune-bashing excursion was completely immersive. The earthy smell of the desert. Our stomachs dropping through the floorboard. Our lungs gasping for air in between laughs and screams. Sweat dripping down our backs from the heat. It was a truly unforgettable experience.

The dunes were just the beginning. Dubai is a sensory wonderland. Imagine a mix of Las Vegas and Miami . . . *times ten*. It has more thousand-foot skyscrapers than New York and more miles of sandy beaches than LA. During the day, we dipped our toes in the Persian Gulf while the kids played in the waves. In the evening, we went into the city and participated in the beautiful, colorful, and intoxicating Ramadan celebration. (We're Catholic, but my wife and I grew up in the Middle East and have deep respect for these Islamic traditions.) Dancers flowed through the crowd like water. Musicians played lively music as the smell of food from a thousand iftars (the evening meal that ends the day of fasting) made our mouths water. The air was cool and the night sky was a deep indigo. Strangers became family. It was like living in a dream. We were mesmerized.

Dubai felt like home—so much so that we decided to move there in 2022. It's immersive yet relaxing; exciting but also welcoming; above all, it feels like a community.

In our age of Zoom webinars and networking, it's easy to forget what a real community feels like. It's not just an activity, it's an experience—one that delights *all* the senses and bonds you to the people around you. This is the type of community we should strive to create, no matter our field or industry.

Here's how.

DELIGHTING THE SENSES

The bar has never been higher for creating engaging experiences. Communities now compete with the most fascinating, colorful, exciting, and addicting content of all time. How can a virtual webinar stand a chance? Why would someone travel cross-country for a weekend con-ference when they can meet ten times more people in a Discord chat?

Luckily, community builders still have evolutionary biology on our side. Human brains still prefer immersive *experiences* over consuming things on a screen.

Jonathan Yaffe, co-founder of the experience man-agement platform, AnyRoad, defines an experience as something that stimulates at least three senses. By this definition, your typical Zoom webinar is not an experi-ence because it only engages sight and sound. Compare that to video games, which incorporate the senses of touch and movement (called the vestibular sense). Compare *that* to wandering the streets of Dubai during Ramadan, which stimulates all those, plus your senses of smell, taste, movement, and connection. There are levels to the immersiveness of an experience, and it all comes down to how many senses are being stimulated at once.

In the startup world, there are experiences, and then there are *immersive* experiences—the kind that leave a tattoo on your heart and change who you are. On the lower end of the immersiveness spectrum, you have pitch competitions. Unless you're the one pitching, these aren't very immersive. There may be food and drinks, inter-esting conversations and compelling presentations, but you're still just a spectator. You aren't actively involved in the event.

Then there are hackathons. These events throw you right into the action. Over the course of twelve to twen-ty-four hours, you'll work side by side with other engineers to build something awesome. It's active, engaging, and a great way to make new friends.

And then there's Startup Weekend.

Startup Weekend, which is now run by Techstars, is like a hackathon and a pitch competition rolled into one and crammed into a seventy-two-hour ultra-marathon. To start, participants meet as a single group and share their one-sentence startup ideas. They write these ideas on a sticky note and place them on a wall. Then all the participants vote on which ideas they like best. The top five to ten ideas are chosen, then folks split up into groups to start building. Over the next three days, teams work together to bring their startup to life, including a minimal viable product, business plan, go-to-market strategy, and investment pitch. On Sunday, the teams present their businesses and compete for startup glory (and, if they're lucky, real investment money).

Startup Weekend's an absurd amount of work for such a short period of time . . . and that's the point. It doesn't just engage all the senses—it cranks the stimulation up all the way to ten. Participants stay up all night, fueled by free energy drinks and coffee. As teams race toward the finish line, the project becomes all consuming—the team enters a collective flow state while the smell of pizza hangs in the air. You hear the chatter of product teams, the clicking of developers on keyboards, and the occasional buzz saw as a team builds a physical prototype. For the participants, win or lose, it's an experience they'll never forget.

Not only is Startup Weekend insanely immersive—it's inexpensive and dead simple to run. It proves you don't need a massive budget or complex logistics to create a world-class experience. All you need is a large space, strong Wi-Fi, and a few dozen pizzas (something I know well). You don't have to splurge on a top-end conference center or keynote speakers. You're feeding people at $2 a head instead of $50. Despite the low overhead, Startup Weekend is one of the best startup community events in the world.

Whether your events are digital, in-person, or somewhere in the middle, there are always ways to elevate your community experience and delight your members.

But before we get to that, let me answer a question you may be asking: Is all this effort to create immersive experiences really worth it?

THE POWER OF EXPERIENCES

Engaging multiple senses to delight your members is not a gimmick—it's not even a luxury. It's an *essential* part of creating community experiences.

And the research proves it.

Aradhna Krishna runs the Sensory Marketing Lab at the University of Michigan. She studies the power of sensory experiences on influencing human behavior, particularly in marketing. In a study first reported in the

Harvard Business Review, Krishna's team found that engaging multiple senses (when combined in a congruent way) has a compounding effect on the overall experience. In other words, for every extra sensation you engage, the experience becomes exponentially better.

What's even more interesting is that your use of multisensory experiences goes largely unnoticed. People don't view Red Bull sporting events as marketing. They're just having a great time, and as a result, they're falling in love with the brand. The impact is subconscious. That's why experiential marketing is so powerful—when customers don't perceive something as marketing, they let their defenses down. Experiential marketing will work forever, so long as the experiences continue to impress.

This research is critical for community leaders to understand and use. It means that every extra effort to engage your members has an outsized impact on their overall experience—even if they don't consciously recognize it.

Let's go back to SaaStr, the world's largest community for business software leaders. The SaaStr Conference is one of my all-time favorite events because they nail *every* detail, big and small. When dreaming up the SaaStr Conference, founder Jason Lemkin didn't want to create just another tech event; he took inspiration from music festivals like Coachella and Burning Man. Instead of renting a conference hall, SaaStr is hosted outdoors in beautiful Santa Clara, California. The carnival-like atmosphere makes you forget you're at a work event. The warm sunshine is relaxing, the DJ set is stimulating, and you're surrounded by strangers who instantly become friends. As an ode to Burning Man, SaaStr even has a giant robot statue that rides around on a trolley and doubles as a light-up dance floor.

You can't point to any single detail that makes SaaStr great. It's the collective experience: the labyrinth of speakers, games, and music; beer gardens for networking; brain dates for spontaneous new connections; and every type of food under the sun. At SaaStr 2021, I rode from booth to booth on a scooter, making friends and chatting up vendors. It was so much fun, I forgot I was working. Yet from a networking and relationship standpoint, it was one of the most productive weeks of the year.

SaaStr continues to set the bar higher every year. The rest of us are just trying to catch up!

Speaking of Burning Man, we can take a lot of inspiration from one of the most immersive experiences in the world. The iconic event in the Nevada desert has been a cultural touchstone for free spirits and creatives (and more recently, Silicon Valley techies) for decades. Attendees come together to create Black Rock City, "a temporary metropolis dedicated to community, art, self-expression, and participation," says the official website. "In this crucible of creativity, all are welcome."

The event's centerpiece is a massive wooden sculpture of a human, which is—spoiler alert—*burned* on the last night of the event.

But Burning Man isn't just a show for pyromaniacs. The entire experience is designed to encourage individuals to express themselves in ways they may not be able to in everyday life. People create art installations, put on performances, and attend workshops on everything from intention-setting to wine tasting. Attendees are divided into camps who each create a unique theme for their impromptu community. Camps eat, dance, and meditate together. They build mutant vehicles and ride together across the barren landscape. The experience is other-worldly. For many Burning Man attendees, it changes their lives forever.

Now that you're inspired to think big, let's break down how to design an immersive, multisensory experience, step by step.

HOW TO DESIGN A MULTISENSORY EXPERIENCE

AnyRoad, the experiential marketing platform co-founded by Jonathan Yaffe, helps companies like Red Bull and Diageo to measure the effectiveness of brand activations (a fancy term for events). While these brands were built on live events, they realized very quickly in the COVID-19 pandemic that they had to transition to digital. They were pleasantly surprised that, when done right, digital activations could be nearly as effective as their physical counterparts. Again, the key is how many senses you're able to engage.

Whether you're hosting digital events, in-person meetups, or hybrid events, it's vital to turn your activity into a multisensory experience. If you don't, you risk losing your members' interest, and eventually their support.

But you can't just blow up a bouncy castle, turn on some music, and call it an "experience" (unless you're hosting a five-year-old's birthday). Like Professor Krishna's research suggested, the senses you engage need to be congruent—not just with one another, but with your community's purpose and your members' goals.

STEP 1: START WITH THE END IN MIND

Immersive experiences don't happen by accident. Start by imagining the type of impression you want to make on your members—not just what they'll do or learn, but how they'll *feel* at the end. What emotions do you want to evoke? What types of relationships do you want members to create? What is the *transformation* they will undergo?

At our 2019 Traction Conf Opening Reception in the Chinese Garden, we wanted members to walk away feeling refreshed, focused, and optimistic. We didn't want folks to network, but forge real relationships. The environment for this event played a huge role in rejuvenating our busy guests and allowing them to create meaningful connections.

Compare this experience to SaaStr. Jason Lemkin wants attendees to leave the conference feeling like they just had the best weekend of their lives . . . at a business conference! The vibe is completely different, but both are immersive experiences in their own way.

So before you rent a giant robot dance floor, think about the end state you want to create for your members, then work backward to build it.

STEP 2: RESEARCH EXPERIENCES *OUTSIDE* YOUR INDUSTRY

Once you know the end state you want to create, it's time to brainstorm ideas. But don't copy other events in your industry. Strive to create something totally unique for your members by looking outside your normal domain.

In my opinion, modeling the SaaStr conference after Burning Man and Coachella is pure brilliance. But you can find inspiration anywhere. Sometimes, you just need to look up. The local Atlassian community in Dubai hosts networking dinners in gorgeous locations around the city, including a forty-three-story sky lounge in the center of the financial district. The event feels like something straight out of a James Bond movie, not a digital ops community. The Dubai chapter leaders want to create a feeling of success and exclusivity for their group. Everyone who attends feels like a "who's who" as they gaze across the gorgeous Dubai skyline.

Personally, I find inspiration everywhere I travel. Whether it's Dubai during Ramadan or a Kenyan safari excursion, you'll never be short of ideas if you expose yourself to the world.

Seek inspiration everywhere you go. Remember, don't stop at what your members expect. Go above and beyond to blow them away.

STEP 3: CREATE A SENSE MAP

Let's get into the nitty gritty. You know the end state you're trying to create and have an exciting idea for your event. Now let's make sure you're engaging as many senses as possible by using a *sense map*. A sense map is simply a list of the seven human senses and how you plan to engage each one.

Our seven senses include:

+ Sight
+ Sound
+ Smell
+ Taste
+ Touch
+ Movement (i.e., vestibular)
+ Place and connection (i.e., proprioception)

Here's an example of a sense map for our Traction Conf Opening Reception at the Chinese Garden.

ENSE		HOW TO EVOKE	COSTS
SIGHT		Bright green vegetation; colorful flowers; a circular path inviting you to walk around and explore.	Free $$$$
SOUND		The DJ playing mellow EDM beats; the sizzle of steak on the grill; soft conversation all around you; the occasional fit of laughter sparked by a new friendship.	$$
SMELL		A freshly watered garden; flowers in full bloom; the crisp air of Vancouver summer; the mouthwatering smell of grilled meat, spicy noodles, and savory vegetables.	Free $$$$
TASTE		The best food you'll ever eat at a business conference.	$$
TOUCH		Warm hugs from friends; relaxed handshakes from new acquaintances; a pat on the back from the host.	Free
MOVEMENT		Walking around the circular garden; alternating sips of wine and bites of egg roll.	Free $$$$
PLACE & CONNECTION		New friends; new memories; an unforgettable environment.	Free

as possible. As you engage more senses, the quality of the experience compounds exponentially.

STEP 4: *EVOKE* THE SENSES YOU CAN'T PHYSICALLY ENGAGE

If your community is primarily online, you might look at the sense map above think, "How on earth can you engage the sense of smell during a webinar?"

Here's the secret to engaging multiple senses online: you don't have to physically stimulate each sense; you can *evoke* the senses in the minds of your members.

Don't believe me? Let me quickly tell you about my favorite dessert. Imagine this . . .

A warm, rich chocolate molten lava cake, still so hot you can see steam rising from it. On top is a mound of luscious vanilla ice cream that's already melting down the sides of the cake. I use my fork to slice open the gooey dessert. A tsunami of liquified chocolate floods my plate and its scent fills my nostrils. The first bite is a perfect mix of cake, molten chocolate, and cold, sweet ice cream. I'm in heaven.

My mouth literally started to water as I wrote that. How about you?

In their book, *The Experience Economy*, Joseph Pine and James Gilmore share how brands evoke our senses all the time, even in online interactions. Why do you think restaurants spend so much energy on their Instagram feeds? Videos and images today are so high quality, they literally trick your brain into thinking there's a juicy, steaming cheeseburger sitting right in front of you. (Sorry, I'll stop with the food talk now.)

You can evoke other senses as well, like the sense of touch. Apple does this brilliantly with photography. They use stunning, high-resolution photos to show off their products on billboards, in stores, and online. These photos are taken from multiple angles and juxtaposed against high-contrast backdrops to make the devices pop. You can practically *feel* the smooth aluminum frame of the Apple Watch when looking at a photo online. These influences are subtle, which is exactly why they are so powerful.

For online and hybrid communities, one of the most important senses to evoke is proprioception. Physically, proprioception refers to the sense of feeling your body in space. If you close your eyes, you can still sense where your hands, feet, and legs are in relation to the rest of your body. Sensory deprivation tanks, which are sometimes used to enhance meditation, remove your sense of proprioception by having you float in a pool of salt water in pitch-black darkness. You literally can't feel your body; a unique experience to say the least.

We also experience a kind of *social* proprioception when we feel connected to others. We can evoke a sense of closeness between community members by allowing time to connect one-on-one and build personal relationships. Even if you're not physically in the same room, you can still feel close to someone by having a meaningful conversation.

Another way to create a sense of closeness in online spaces is to encourage participants to "share" a meal together. At a virtual Traction meetup in 2020, I sent

Uber Eats gift cards to online participants so they could buy lunch during the event. Even though we were all separated, we kindled meaningful connections over food—a deeply human tradition.

As you fill out your sense map, don't let physical or digital limitations hold you back. Use your imagination—and a healthy dose of evocative photography and video—to engage as many senses as possible.

STEP 5: CRANK EACH SENSE WAY UP

Unfortunately, in such a noisy world, subtlety rarely stands out. Don't be understated when engaging the senses. Crank them way up. Even if you're just hosting a pizza party, make sure it's the best damn pizza your members have ever had. If you're trying to create a sense of calm and optimism, book the most serene venue in the city. Don't just host another networking dinner—be like the Dubai Atlassian community and dine among the skyscrapers.

"Designing experience is theater," said Joseph Pine in *The Experience Economy*.

Dubai is a city that fully embraces this concept. They didn't just build a tall skyscraper—they built the tallest in the world! They also built the world's tallest observation wheel, the world's deepest scuba diving pool, and a giant set of manmade islands shaped like a palm. After decades of reliance on oil money, the government has been rebuilding their economy around amazing cultural experiences. From the food to attractions to the incredibly cool Museum of the Future, the entire city is designed to inspire awe. Even the taxi drivers go above and beyond to make great conversation. It's a city with a singular goal: to make you feel like you're part of the community.

At Traction Conf, we go above and beyond every chance we get. We don't just play music in between keynotes—we have our own theme song. It was written by a Traction member who also happens to be a rapper. (You can still find the song on his Soundcloud. Thanks, Smixx!) We play it during virtual events as well to connect the entire Traction experience.

STEP 6: BUDGETING—EFFORT VS. IMPACT

At this point you may be thinking, "This all sounds great, Lloyed, but I don't have the budget to create multisensory experiences like these."

Money is certainly a concern you need to address. Most of us don't have the budget of a SaaStr, and certainly not Apple. That doesn't mean you can't create incredible and immersive experiences. In fact, we still run Traction Conf as lean as possible because it still needs to turn a profit. It's not just a marketing channel like some business conferences backed by multibillion-dollar corporations. As we saw with Startup Weekend, it doesn't have to cost you a fortune to create an immersive experience.

At Boast.AI, we lost a major sense of community during the COVID-19 pandemic when everyone went remote. We combatted this by hosting virtual fitness classes for employees. We made them simple enough for anyone to join, regardless of fitness level. Then we gamified it by creating a points system and adding prize tiers. Finally, whoever led the most recent fitness class would nominate the next leader, who would create their own workout for us to tackle. It was easy to set up and exponentially better than Zoom happy hours so many companies tried to run. The sense of movement turned it into a bona fide experience.

When the budget is tight, go back to your Why. Remember the purpose of your community—why members are gathering in the first place. Create events and activities that center on your core values, and engage multiple senses to heighten the experience.

GO ABOVE AND BEYOND

What would your community look like if you stopped hosting events and started creating experiences?

The first thing you'd notice is a deeper sense of connection between members. Humans bond over shared experiences, not shared Zoom calls. A digital meetup with an added physical or gastronomical component is much better for building relationships.

When genuine connections are being made, you'll see your community retention rates rise. People are starving for meaningful experiences these days; if you can provide that, you'll create members for life. But that's not all. Happy members attract more like-minded members, and suddenly your community will be growing on its own. This is the definition of community-led growth. You might even be able to expand your community to new groups of people, like HubSpot was able to do with sales and customer success professionals.

Create cultural touchpoints for your members—unforgettable experiences that fulfill them and keep them coming back for more. But you don't have to do this all on your own.

In the next rule, we'll talk about involving your members to create even better community experiences.

RULE 9:

COLLABORATE WITH YOUR COMMUNITY

"THEY DON'T JUST GIVE FEEDBACK, THEY TAKE INITIATIVE AND BUILD THE DAMN THING THEMSELVES."

LOTS OF COMPANIES say they're community-led. But few put their values into practice when things go wrong.

Or in the case of GitLab on January 31, 2017—horribly, catastrophically wrong.

GitLab is an enterprise DevOps platform founded in 2014. That means other tech companies build, host, and run their software on GitLab. They are a core piece of infrastructure for some of the world's largest companies. So when GitLab went offline for nearly twelve hours in early 2017, it wasn't just a big deal. It could have ended the startup's existence.

Problems started around 9:20 a.m. Pacific time on January 31, when a few users started spamming the GitLab forums, which caused a slowdown. This is not an unusual problem and the company had protocols to deal with it. But humans are, well, human, and mistakes happen. In an effort to remove the spammers, a GitLab systems administrator accidentally deleted some data from GitLab's production servers (i.e., the live, public servers). Bad luck struck twice when the backup systems failed at the same time. This started an emergency at GitLab—the kind many companies don't bounce back from. Not only did GitLab.com go offline for hours, but the company permanently lost customer data. This is a cardinal sin in the world of tech infrastructure. Around 5,000 GitLab projects were impacted.

At this time, GitLab was a three-year-old startup in a highly competitive market. They were just beginning to move into the enterprise space, which came with loads of risk on its own. This incident, which one tech media outlet described as a "meltdown," could have ended the company for good. I'm sure their competitors were eagerly watching as their biggest rival burned to the ground.

But GitLab did not go under. In fact, they flipped the potential disaster into a major win. How on earth did they pull it off?

One word: collaboration.

You see, GitLab is not your typical tech startup. They are an open core company, which means their core technology is open sourced on the web. Open source is the practice of letting anyone contribute to your code base. GitLab's core technology is completely free for anyone in the world to use. They make money by building premium and enterprise support features for large companies.

As part of their open-source ethos, one of GitLab's core values is collaboration. They involve their community in everything from designing features to shipping security patches each month. Some people think this open-source policy hurts GitLab because it exposes their work to hackers and competitors. In reality, collaboration makes them flexible and resilient.

Resilient enough to survive the database meltdown of 2017.

GitLab is a shining example of a company that continued practicing their values in the most dire of times. In their darkest moment, they didn't batten down the hatches and go silent. They became even more collaborative as they worked around the clock to fix the issue:

TRANSPARENCY: GitLab was transparent about the incident from the start, sharing detailed updates on the company's blog, Twitter, and a status page. The updates included information about what caused the issue, how GitLab was working to fix it, and how customers could keep track of the situation. The transparency helped build trust with the community and showed that GitLab was taking the issue seriously.

CODE CONTRIBUTIONS: GitLab actively encouraged its community members to contribute to the recovery effort. Customers were encouraged to open up issues on GitLab's instance and provide feedback, bug reports, and suggestions. GitLab also provided a public spreadsheet where customers could report any data loss, which allowed the company to more quickly assess the extent of the damage. For example, a community member created a script that allowed customers to recover their lost data from their own GitLab instances.

PUBLIC HACKATHON: GitLab organized a public hackathon to address the issues that arose from the database meltdown. The hackathon was open to anyone who wanted to participate, and over five hundred people did. Participants worked on fixing bugs, improving the documentation, and developing new features. GitLab also set up a Slack channel specifically for the hackathon, where community members could work directly with GitLab employees.

POST-MORTEM ANALYSIS: After the incident was resolved, GitLab conducted a thorough post-mortem analysis and shared the results with its community. The analysis included a detailed explanation of what happened, what went wrong, and what steps GitLab was taking to prevent similar incidents from happening in the future. GitLab also shared a list of lessons learned, which included things like the importance of testing backups regularly and making sure that all staff members know how to respond in a crisis.

When other companies would have tried to control the narrative, GitLab opened their doors and invited the world in. The response? Near-universal praise, appreciation, and forgiveness. Here are a few comments left on the company blog:

"Everybody makes mistakes, but what we learn from them defines experience."

"Thank you for sharing your experience and helping people benefit from your mistakes, it takes tremendous courage and as such you have my utmost respect."

"You guys are awesome. Thanks for sharing your mistakes and allowing us to learn from you."

"Sh*t happens, huge props for being transparent as ever! Makes waiting easier. Virtual cup of coffee for your engineers!"

The GitLab community stepped up to help in any way they could. Their slogan became "Keep Calm and GitLab on." One community member even offered to fly to GitLab's headquarters to help in person.

In under twenty-four hours, the restoration process was complete with minimal damage or loss of data. Because of GitLab's commitment to collaboration, they not only weathered this storm, but came out better and stronger because of it.

DON'T BUILD ALONE

Control is an intoxicating drug. Even the most community-centric leaders sometimes crave the power of a command-and-control model. It makes things simple. Easy. But also fragile.

For many first-time community builders, control is the only thing they know. They want the community experience to be perfect, so they try to orchestrate every single detail themselves. But by holding on to control, these leaders are depriving themselves—and their members—of a community's most powerful force: the ability to work together to solve problems and create experiences. At some point or another, every successful community leader learns this lesson: in order to grow, you have to let go.

A strong community is one where members feel a sense of autonomy for the success of the group. They take matters into their own hands, often improving the communities in ways the leadership team could never imagine. Take Startup Grind, for example. At Traction Conf 2019, founder Derek Andersen told the story of the local Startup Grind chapter in Babol, a 250,000-person city on the Caspian coast of

Iran. Not only did the SG team *not* start that chapter, they didn't even know it existed! They only learned about it when the Babol group posted photos online from a recent event. By leaving room for collaboration, the SG community expanded and improved on its own.

Another example comes from Duolingo, the most popular language-learning app in the U.S. Unlike other language-learning systems, Duolingo has courses for some of the world's rarest languages, including Gaelic, Latin, and Native Hawaiian. They even have fictional languages like High Valyrian (*Game of Thrones*) and Klingon (*Star Trek*). How could a company dedicate resources to a language like Basque, which is collectively spoken by less than a million people?

Easy. They crowdsourced it.

When Duolingo was founded in 2012, they started a program called the Incubator, where volunteer linguists could create language courses on the platform. The Incubator was a massive boost for Duolingo, which quickly developed the most diverse set of language lessons in the world. It only took one person interested in teaching Navajo to start the Navajo course track. As a language gained popularity, the company's internal linguistics team would grow and support it.

Duolingo set clear guidelines for developing language courses that met their quality standards and teaching methodology (e.g., contextual learning instead of grammar-based lessons). Today, the Duolingo community is richer, more diverse, and more valuable because the company involved their community.

SIX STEPS FOR COMMUNITY COLLABORATION

Some leaders think community involvement always *devolves* into chaos and anarchy. I understand where they're coming from, but I believe that says more about the leader than it does about the community. Yes, collaborating with your members requires trust between leadership and the general population. But then again, what community *doesn't* rely on trust? If you don't trust members to take ownership of the community, I believe there are deeper issues that you need to address.

That said, I'm confident you are a trusting leader and eager to collaborate with your members. Let's look at how:

1. Align on Values
2. Build Trust through Transparency
3. Focus on Your Zone of Genius
4. Set Guidelines (Not Rules)
5. Create a Clear Path for Involvement
6. Find and Empower Your Superfans

STEP 1: ALIGN ON VALUES

When you gather with your community under one roof (physically or metaphorically), there will always be differences in personality and interests. Clearly defined values are what will create shared common ground for your community.

GitLab, for example, has six core values:

+ Collaboration
+ Results
+ Efficiency
+ Diversity, inclusion, and belonging
+ Iteration
+ Transparency

These values are clearly outlined and explained in the GitLab handbook (more on this incredible resource later). Not only do these values allow GitLab members to self-select into the community, they also allow the community to hold GitLab leadership accountable. GitLab (the company) has no room to flake on their values without being called out by GitLab (the community).

But GitLab's values also serve as a powerful decision-making framework for members and leadership alike. Take the database meltdown of 2017, for example. Since collaboration and transparency are core values, running a hackathon was an easy decision.

If you have not yet defined and publicly shared your community values, I recommend doing this asap. Refer back to Rule 3 to find your powerful Why. You'll be astounded by the results. Like Derek Andersen discovered after posting Startup Grind's values on their website, you will start to attract like-minded members like thirsty lions to water. And when problems arise in the community, your values will guide you and your members to address them—together.

STEP 2: BUILD TRUST THROUGH TRANSPARENCY

Trust is the cornerstone of all relationships. And one of the best ways to build trust is through transparency.

In the book *Small Giants: Companies That Choose to Be Great Instead of Big*, author Bo Burlingham tells the story of a small pizza chain in the Chicago suburbs called Nick's Pizza & Pub. Nick's was a beloved establishment in the community, but a series of bad luck—and an over-leveraged credit line—led to an existential crisis for the company in 2011. The restaurant was $3 million in debt and losing $30,000 per month. New store openings were put on hold due to lack of funds. Founder Nick Sarillo estimated the company would not even be able to make payroll in one month's time. He was out of options . . . except one:

Transparency.

Against the advice of his friends, family, counsel, and business partners, Sarillo sent a last-ditch email to his customers. He explained their financial situation in detail, took full responsibility for the mistakes he had made, and asked for their help to generate more revenue over the next several weeks. The response surprised everyone at the company—especially Sarillo. Within five minutes of sending the email, the phone at Nick's Pizza & Pub started ringing off the hook. Fans started a "Save Nick's Pizza" Facebook page and scheduled pizza parties. Businesses booked Nick's for banquets, and two national TV stations picked up the story. Sales doubled the following week and remained at that level for the next five weeks. Nick's made payroll and avoided bankruptcy. The boost in sales gave Sarillo time to create a new business plan with the help of a local accountant who agreed to work pro bono. The crisis was averted—and the company came out better because of it.

Don't take away the wrong lesson from this story. You should always be transparent with your community, not just during times of crisis. GitLab's track record of transparency is why their customers trusted them to fix the problems they faced during the database meltdown. Trust is built in good times and relied upon in bad times. Make sure you fill up your trust tank during the good times for when (not *if*) things go wrong.

STEP 3: FOCUS ON YOUR ZONE OF GENIUS

Building and running a community takes a lot of work. As you look for ways to involve your community, focus on your personal strengths and outsource the rest.

John Kim, the founder and CEO of Sendbird, shared his thoughts on delegation with me during a Traction webinar. He said that founders tend to freak out when it's finally time to give up control. They're used to doing everything themselves, but holding on to control is the best way to stall the growth of your business or community.

So how do you find the right balance of control and delegation?

First, identify your ideal role in building the community. What do you do best? What do you enjoy doing most? Where these two questions overlap is your *zone of genius*. Pick one or two things that fall in your zone of genius and hold on to those tasks. Now delegate the rest to your team (if you have one), or find community members willing to volunteer. This is easier said than done, of course, but this exercise will at least help you identify what roles you need help filling.

At Traction, my zone of genius is building relationships with founders, partners, and speakers. My most important job is to fill up our podcast and event lineups with startup rockstars. For everything else—from event logistics to communications to podcast editing—I find help. Where did the best candidates for these roles come from? You already know the answer: the community! Hiring from your community means they are already aligned on your big Why. You can be confident they will buy into your purpose and give you their best every day.

Whether you're hiring full-time staff or looking for community volunteers, the process is the same: identify your zone of genius, then seek out help for the rest.

STEP 4: SET GUIDELINES, NOT RULES

Companies set rules and policies to direct employee behavior. With communities, you need a softer touch.

Everyone is voluntarily spending their time with you, so strict policies are more likely to drive members away (the exception being rules on safety and etiquette).

Instead, establish guidelines for member contributions and collaboration. What's the difference between a policy and a guideline? A policy says you need to post three comments per week in the Discord to keep your membership. A guideline shows you *how* to publish a positive and engaging comment.

When Duolingo started crowdsourcing its language courses, they didn't tell community members how many courses to create or what lessons to build. Instead, they gave their volunteer linguists a set of guidelines for creating effective courses. They taught creators the contextual learning methodology, which relies on real-life experiences instead of grammar lessons. Outside of that, creators could make lessons however they wanted. This guideline resulted in some hilarious language lessons, like this Norwegian phrase: "Jeg spiser brød og gråter på gulvet." ("I am eating bread and crying on the floor.")

Not only did Duolingo's guidelines encourage member involvement, it actually made the community more interesting and vibrant.

STEP 5: CREATE A CLEAR PATH FOR INVOLVEMENT

You'll have many members eager to get involved, but you need to give them a clear path to do so. Show them exactly how they can get involved at each stage of the community. Make it easy to make an impact right away.

For an open-source product like GitLab, community collaboration is mission critical to their business, so they don't leave anything up to chance. They created the GitLab Heroes program to gamify involvement and reward their top volunteers. After five code contributions, three blog posts, or organizing a GitLab event, volunteers reach the rank of Contributor. At this stage, they are rewarded with GitLab swag, personal support from the GitLab team, and public shoutouts on GitLab social media. The next level up is the GitLab Hero. Heroes get an unlimited GitLab license for personal use, invites to conferences, and even more personalized support. The top contributors are called Superheroes. These superfans receive direct access to the GitLab team and personalized coaching to build their careers as tech evangelists.

If you want to be involved at GitLab, there is a crystal-clear roadmap to follow. Create your own roadmap to encourage the type of contributions you want in your community.

STEP 6: FIND AND EMPOWER YOUR SUPERFANS

Even with a clear path for involvement, not every community member will take it. Most will live somewhere between lurker and occasional participant. This is totally normal, but that means you need to find and empower the few members who are true champions.

Every successful community has fans. These are the folks who show up to every event, respond to your emails, and buy your merch. But then there are the super-fans—your champions—the ones who would get a tattoo of your logo on their shoulder. They don't just attend events; they drag their friends and colleagues along with them. They don't just give feedback on what would make the community better; they take initiative and build the damn thing themselves.

If you have superfans in your community, do any-thing you can to get them involved. Give them leader-ship responsibility as a mentor, lead volunteer, chapter leader, or moderator. Startup Grind, for example, never struggles to find chapter leaders and event volunteers. Any time there's a need for help, their superfans step up. We've also experienced this at Traction Conf. If I notice a member participating heavily in our virtual events, I'll reach out personally to ask if they'd like to volunteer at the in-person Traction Conf. Their reward is more than a free ticket; volunteers get inside access to the speakers, after-parties, and behind-the-scenes workings of events. It's a position with lots of perks—exactly the kind of perks your superfans care about.

This step is so important that we dedicated an entire rule to it. That's next.

RULE 10:

REWARD YOUR CHAMPIONS

"THEY ARE MISSION CRITICAL FOR BUILDING A THRIVING COMMUNITY."

HUBSPOT HAS OVER 158,000 customers. But just a fraction are true champions of the brand. And without these champions, there's a chance we would have never heard of HubSpot in the first place.

HubSpot Solutions Partners make up less than 4 percent of all HubSpot customers, yet they are responsible for 40 percent of the company's revenue. Other SaaS platforms would call them "resellers," but HubSpot Partners do so much more than that. They help other businesses grow with sales, marketing, e-commerce, and customer support services—all while using the HubSpot platform. The more successful HubSpot Partners are, the more successful HubSpot will be.

HubSpot knows their champions are mission critical to the company's success, and they reward them with one of the most generous partner programs in business. To start, all Partners earn 20 percent commission on HubSpot revenue they generate for three years. With the average HubSpot customer spending over $11,000 per year, this quickly adds up to a significant income stream.

The very best HubSpot Partners get even more. As Partners sell and manage more HubSpot business, they earn tiers that unlock new benefits. Tiered partners are prominently listed in HubSpot's vendor directory, get priority support, access to sales and marketing tools, invites to exclusive events, and much more. As they climb the ranks of Gold, Platinum, Diamond, and Elite tiers, the perks get better. There are about 1,100 tiered HubSpot Partners in the world—less than 1 percent of all HubSpot customers, but certainly the most impactful.

HubSpot's obsession with rewarding its champions is more than a business decision. It's part of the company's core philosophy. Slide twenty-five of HubSpot's Culture Code reads: "We believe success is making those who believed in you look brilliant." HubSpot Partners believe deeply in the platform. In return, HubSpot rewards them with world-class tools *and* world-class compensation. HubSpot Partners drive HubSpot success and vice versa. It's a win-win.

Every community has champions. They are the most powerful force in community-led growth. Are you properly incentivizing them? What more could you do to activate this incredible asset?

Before we answer those questions, let's dig into just how important your community champions really are.

THE 1-9-90 PRINCIPLE

Champions don't just improve your community. They *make* your community. Literally. Most communities would cease to exist without their superfans.

Case in point: Yelp.

Yelp is a review and recommendation platform for restaurants and services. Home services are their fastest growing category, but they're arguably best known for food reviews, so let's focus on that.

Unlike Zagat, MICHELIN, or Eater, Yelp reviews don't come from food critics or journalists; they're created by regular customers. Yelp users take photos, give star ratings, and write descriptive reviews for the next diner. Yelp has turned reviewing into a game by rewarding users with status and influence.

But the entire game would fall apart if it weren't for their most active users. Yelp realized early on that fanatical reviewers were the backbone of their business. As a social network, Yelp's user base naturally follows the 1-9-90 rule of online participation: 90 percent of your users are lurkers (aka, pure consumers), 9 percent are occasional contributors, and 1 percent are frequent content creators.

Yelp's top 1 percent of users created nearly *all* the content on its site.

Before becoming Duolingo's Head of Community, Laura Nestler crafted the community growth playbook at Yelp. Her strategy was simple: "We could win if we spent all our energy identifying a very small group of fanatic reviewers," she said at Traction Conf 2019. "They were driving our value."

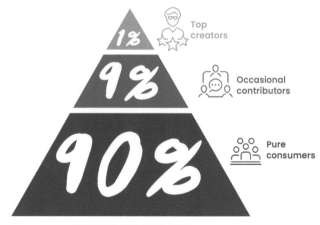

Source: Charles Arthur, 2006

Most growth marketers focus on their total addressable market. Nestler and her team did the opposite. They didn't worry about the 99 percent of consumers and casual contributors. Yelp focused on getting its top users to write more reviews. They used a blend of extrinsic and intrinsic motivators to drive more content. One of the key perks was the Yelp Elite Squad (YES! for short). Every city had a local YES! chapter, an invite-only community for Yelp's top users. They held private, exclusive events for YES! members and their friends. It became a status symbol and also a tight-knit social circle. Yelp rewarded its champions with friendships, influence, access, and respect.

In hindsight, the 1-9-90 strategy seems obvious for a company like Yelp. But many of Yelp's competitors took different (and arguably worse) approaches to growing their platforms. *Food and Wine* magazine organizes massive food festivals around the world (in addition to its content business). Time Out has built food halls in major cities that feature the region's best restaurants. MICHELIN, Zagat, Eater, and media outlets hire massive teams of restaurant reviewers and content creators. Each of these approaches is focused on the target market as a whole, while Yelp invested in its champions.

As a result, Yelp is worth over $2 billion while its competitors are worth just a fraction of that (Time Out is the only other publicly traded company we researched. At the time of this writing, it was worth around $136 million). It's an impressive feat in an industry plagued by low profits and aggressive acquisitions.

Every community has their own version of the 1-9-90 rule. The vast majority of your community's activity—whether it be content, event attendance, or code contributions—will be generated by a small minority of superfans. Without them, your community will grind to a halt. This is why rewarding your champions is *mission critical*. Yelp provides the blueprint: identify your top users and reward them with a blend of intrinsic and extrinsic motivators.

Let's look at four ways to reward your champions for their efforts.

CREATE OPPORTUNITIES FOR GROWTH

Your top 1 percent fans want to be involved in every possible way. Not only do they want to see the community succeed, they're driven by opportunities for personal growth, professional development, and status. How can you help them get what they want?

Traction has about 110,000 subscribers, but only a hundred or so volunteer for Traction Conf every year. These are our champions. They put in countless hours of work to make sure our events and programs run smoothly. Without them, it would be impossible for us to offer the kind of high-quality experiences our community expects. Volunteers help with every aspect of our events, from stage management to organizing the niche sessions, working behind the scenes to make sure everything goes off without a hitch. These dedicated volunteers are eager to grow as founders and leaders, which is why they donate their time. We reward them by making them the most plugged-in members of the Traction Community. Many events have industry superstars or the company CEO introduce keynote speakers. At Traction Conf, we give that job over to our volunteers. This gives them a chance to connect face-to-face with industry leaders. We throw an exclusive party for our speakers, investors, special guests, and volunteers. More high-value connections are made at this party than anywhere else in the conference. We reward our volunteers by helping them build their careers. In return, they fuel our community.

Kaggle is one of the best at giving its members opportunities for growth. The data science community has built a collection of over 50,000 datasets and 400,000 public notebooks for use in data analysis projects. Members are rewarded with badges and tiers for their contributions. But Kaggle is best known for their public data science competitions. Anyone can start a competition on Kaggle—from individual contributors to massive corporations like Google—and anyone can participate in solving the challenge. Every competition has a live leaderboard to track the winner, but more importantly, members get to learn and grow alongside the very best data scientists in the world.

GIVE PUBLIC RECOGNITION

It's a universal truth: receiving genuine recognition for your accomplishments feels good. It's one of the most effective and least expensive ways to reward your champions—but some communities go above and beyond.

Reddit is one of the best platforms at publicly recognizing its top users. Unlike other social networks, every Reddit user has a clearly visible score at the top of their profile. Users earn Karma points when their comments and posts are upvoted by other users. You can also send a user Gold for their efforts, which allows them access to members-only channels and removes ads from the platform. Users with higher Karma scores are also more likely to be chosen as channel moderators, and their posts will be taken more seriously.

HubSpot's Impact Awards are all about publicly recognizing HubSpot's best Partners. Impact Awards are for those partners who go above and beyond—not only championing HubSpot, but developing creative solutions for their clients using HubSpot products. Partners can win awards for single-product excellence, platform excellence, technical expertise, DEI (diversity, equity, and inclusion) efforts, and more. Winners are enshrined in HubSpot's Partner Hall of Fame and even win a shiny trophy to display in their offices (or in the background of Zoom calls).

But giving recognition doesn't have to be a big production. Even the smallest forms of public recognition can have a big impact. A simple tactic is to shout out the top contributors each week. At Boast.AI, we made this part of our weekly ritual. We called them Monday MVPs. Each week, employees could nominate someone who made their previous week better. But nominators didn't just submit a name; they drew a picture of their MVP with superhero powers! This little extra effort makes the ritual special. Some people get really creative with the crayons, colored pencils, and Sharpies to bring our superheroes to life. Not only do the MVPs appreciate the recognition, but our nominators love giving it.

Peer-to-peer recognition is often more powerful than top-down recognition because it feels more authentic. Encourage your community to shout out other members of the community. Find your own version of Monday MVPs (or just steal ours! We don't mind sharing).

GIVE MEMBERS A PLATFORM

HubSpot's tiered partner program is based on a generous commission structure designed to help agencies grow their businesses on the HubSpot platform. But HubSpot also empowers its partners to grow their *own* platforms as experts in their domain. Tiered partners are listed prominently in the HubSpot ecosystem directory with their credentials and specialties. On top of that, Diamond and Elite partners get priority to write guest posts on the HubSpot Marketing Blog, which receives hundreds of thousands of visitors a month. This is a massive platform that not only drives new business, but helps partners build authority.

GitLab's Heroes program doesn't pay commissions, but they still give their champions a platform to grow their careers. As an open core company, GitLab relies on technology evangelists to grow their user base. These evangelists are GitLab's top 1 percent, creating loads of content and support for the platform. GitLab's Heroes program is designed to help their biggest champions build their careers as evangelists, which comes with speaking gigs, consulting jobs, and high-paying leadership roles at the world's largest tech companies. They even provide career coaching for their highest-tier Superheroes.

Why would GitLab do so much for such a small segment of users? Because the more successful their champions, the more exposure GitLab gets to new audiences. It's a win-win for the company and their community.

GO OUT OF YOUR WAY TO HELP

One of the simplest but most profound ways to reward your champions is to go out of your way to help them in times of need.

When one of Traction's early champions found herself out of a job, I personally picked up the phone to make introductions for her. I knew she gave 110 percent to everything she did, which included Traction. She quickly found a new job and was a perfect fit.

This may seem like a lot of effort for just one person. But your champions aren't just *any* people. They are *everything* to your community: the creators, the connectors, the energizers. Personally helping *one* champion is the equivalent of helping your entire community.

Communities exist to support their members, but it's your best members who support the community. Go out of your way to reward your champions. Make them feel seen, appreciated, and well compensated for their efforts. Give them opportunities for growth, status, and access. If you take care of your top 1 percent, they will not only be your most active members, but also your biggest cheerleaders.

Happy community champions are mission critical for building a thriving community. Now it's time to build a system around them to keep the rest of your members engaged and entertained.

RULE 11:

MAKE YOUR COMMUNITY STICKY

"THE MOST POWERFUL CORE ACTIONS ARE ELEVATED INTO RITUALS."

PLACED THE QUARTER in the slot and hit *Start*. The ball dropped into place as I pulled back the spring. I took a moment to prepare myself. When I released the lever, the chrome ball shot to life like a racehorse bursting from the starting gate. It circled the table and bounced around faster than my eyes could register. The machine was ablaze with flashing colors and sound. I couldn't take my eyes off the multicolored universe of bells, lights, and buzzers.

As a kid, I was obsessed with pinball. I'd stay at the arcade for hours, playing until long after my hands hurt. But I didn't just play for fun. I wanted to *win*. I had the high scores memorized and was determined to top them each week. Every collision with a flashing bumper meant I was one step closer. I knew where every double and triple score bonus hid on the table, and even how to manipulate the board with a little tilt of the machine. The more I played, the better I got. As my score crept up the leaderboard, I found a sense of flow. I wasn't just playing the game. I *was* the game. Needless to say, I was hooked.

Years later, after co-founding Boast.AI and Traction, I thought back to my early days as a pinball-aholic and I realized the game taught me a valuable lesson: if you can create a highly engaging experience, your best customers and community members will come back again and again.

Every community faces some level of churn. This isn't always a bad thing—some people just don't fit your Ideal

Community Persona. But too much turnover can permanently scar your group and doom it to failure.

The most common reason for churn, in my experience, is treating relationships like transactions. Transactional communities are more focused on new members than existing members. Once someone joins this type of community, they realize the experience is not what was promised. The community leaders are distant and hard to reach. There is little energy among the members. At the same time, you see the community promoting itself and recruiting like crazy, trying to lure that next cohort to keep the lights on.

We've all experienced communities like this: the business conference that promised a high-profile speaker only to have them cancel at the last minute. Or the apartment complex you move into because the leasing agent seemed so friendly, but as soon as you have an issue with the toilet, they're nowhere to be found. Transactional communities can only exist by signing up members faster than they're losing them.

Sarah Tavel, a General Partner at Benchmark, was Pinterest's first product manager from 2012 to 2015. While building Pinterest's community, Tavel had to battle what she calls "empty calories of growth." This is when a community is so focused on new members that they don't realize (or don't care) that they have massive holes further down the funnel. Like eating junk food, empty calories of growth feel great in the beginning, but you eventually pay the price. User acquisition gets more expensive, and you can't keep people on the platform. You eventually enter a death spiral as users start leaving faster than you can replace them.

Like a great product, great communities find a way to keep members around. They become *sticky*. Tavel and her team helped transform Pinterest into one of the most successful social networks in the world. They did this by shipping features to improve Pinterest's core action.

IDENTIFY YOUR CORE ACTION

Sticky communities revolve around a single core action that anchors the member experience. It's so important that your community would cease to exist if members didn't do it. This action is completed so often that it becomes a ritual. It's the community's *raison d'être*—its reason for being.

Pinterest has tons of features. You can comment on posts, share pins with your friends, and set up boards for every aspect of your life. But Pinterest's core action is pinning web pages.

Sarah Tavel and her team focused on improving the pinning experience. They shipped the first recommendations on Pinterest (e.g., related pins, picked for you), improved content search and discovery, and created filters to remove low-quality links from the platform. These improvements made pinning easier and Pinterest stickier.

Harley-Davidson's HOG members get a lot of perks, like discounts on bike insurance, shipping, merchandise, and more. They also participate in philanthropy events and large festivals. But a HOG's core action—the reason it exists—is to go on local group rides. Each HOG chapter hosts rides on a weekly or monthly basis. This is the event where riders build lifelong friendships and memories. A local ride is likely the first event a new HOG member will join. From there, they will go on to participate in the secondary activities that round out the membership experience. But without those regular local rides, HOG members wouldn't stick around for long.

At Traction, our core action is attending live events. Yes, we have a YouTube channel, newsletter, and podcast, but without our in-person events and live webinars, Traction would not exist.

Look at any thriving community and you'll find a clear core action:

+ Duolingo: Take a language lesson
+ Yelp: Leave a restaurant review
+ #NaNoWriMo (National Novel Writing Month): Write a novel
+ Startup Grind: Attend local founder meetups
+ Nas Creator Accelerator: Post a video every week
+ Sales Hacker: Post on the forum

Justin Vogel, the co-founder of Safary, a community of Web3 growth marketers, believes most communities fail by trying to do too much.

"Community builders give their members way too many options for how to engage, and they end up with very little engagement," he said in a Twitter Spaces conversation hosted by Origami.

A community that loses sight of its core action is at risk of falling apart from the inside-out.

TURN YOUR CORE ACTION INTO A RITUAL

The most powerful core actions are elevated into rituals.

Rituals are routine activities that have been imbued with meaning. They are the opposite of mindless habits; rituals inspire contemplation, reflection, and personal growth. They remind you of your Why and connect you to something bigger than yourself. Rituals are an integral part of building authentic connections within your community.

There's no better example of a community built around ritual than CrossFit. The high-intensity, functional movement program is more than a fitness craze. For many members, it's *everything*—their family, social circle, therapy, and spiritual connection. Reading online forums, you'll find testimonials of workouts that make it sound more like a religious experience than a workout.

"CrossFit saves lives" is a common refrain, referring to the company's commitment to fighting entities like the soda industry. "CrossFit is my church" is another popular saying. Phrases like this have led many outsiders to call CrossFit a cult. According to founder Greg Glassman (simply known as "Coach" in the CrossFit world), this isn't a bad thing.

"It's not an insult to a CrossFitter to be called part of a cult," said Glassman in an interview with Casper ter Kuile, author of *The Power of Ritual*. "Discipline, honesty, courage, accountability—what you learn in the gym is also training for life. CrossFit makes better people."

CrossFit turns every activity into a ritual. Their core action is the Workout of the Day (WOD), which members around the world complete. But these are more than workouts. Many are named after deceased members of the community—specifically military members, police officers, firefighters, and other everyday heroes who died in the line of duty. The most famous is The Murph, a workout named in honor of fallen Navy SEAL LT Michael P. Murphy. It's a grueling workout, consisting of a one-mile run, 100 pull-ups, 200 push-ups, 300 squats, and another one-mile run for time.

CrossFit also designates worldwide rest days each week (one might call it a Sabbath). On these days, instead of posting the WOD, CrossFit shares inspirational videos from the community.

On the local level, every CrossFit gym—known as a box—has its own logo and merchandise that members wear with pride. Many boxes hold weekend get-togethers with drinks, karaoke, and talent shows. They celebrate birthdays, anniversaries, and holidays together. The largest event every year is the CrossFit Games, a worldwide competition for the most elite CrossFitters. Local gyms cheer on their hometown champions who qualified to compete, but in the end, it's a celebration of the community as a whole.

"Even though people new to CrossFit often came to lose weight or build muscle," said ter Kuile in *The Power of Rituals,* "what kept them coming back was the deeply engaged and committed community."

CrossFit is one of the best modern examples of how communities become movements, and movements become religions. They use rituals to create meaningful experiences and a sense of purpose. It may seem extreme to outsiders, but Crossfit is far from the only community to do this. Schools hold graduation ceremonies, complete with music, robes, and crossing the threshold as graduates walk across the stage. Online communities—like those found in the Web3 and cryptocurrency worlds—build rituals around memes, running jokes, and greetings like "gm" (short for "good morning"). Cities host festivals, root for the home team, and defend the honor of local delicacies.

If core actions make your community sticky, then rituals make your community a lifestyle.

CREATING VIRTUOUS LOOPS

Every sticky activity in our lives—whether it's a healthy habit or an unhealthy vice—is built on the back of virtuous loops.

A virtuous loop is a cycle of triggers and rewards that encourage us to repeatedly take an action. These actions, in turn, deepen our investment in the activity until it becomes a habit. Virtuous loops can help us form healthy habits like exercise, or they can lead us to eating ice cream every night before bed.

Virtuous loops are also the engines that make communities sticky. Participating in a community is a type of habit, and I believe it's one of the healthiest habits you can build. Communities can change lives by providing connection, purpose, and opportunity.

Nir Eyal is an expert in building virtuous loops. He popularized the strategy of building sticky products and services with his hit book, *Hooked*. Below, I'll share Eyal's Hook framework and how you can use it to build sticky communities.

The Hook Framework:

+ Trigger
+ Action
+ Rewards
+ Investment

Source: Hooked: How to Build Habit-Forming Products by Nir Eyal, NirAndFar.com

TRIGGER

The first step of any virtuous loop is the trigger. A trigger is a call to action, or a reminder for the user to do something. Remember the famous experiment with Pavlov's dogs? The bell was the trigger that made them salivate because they associated it with being fed.

Once you have your core action, you then need to build a trigger to make your members salivate (figuratively speaking, of course).

There are both external and internal triggers. External triggers are reminders from the outside world to do something. Push notifications on your phone are external triggers. So is your alarm clock—a trigger to get out of bed and get ready for work (or to slam that snooze button). For HOG members, external triggers include the monthly HOG magazine they receive in the mail, the email newsletter they get every week, and reminders about upcoming events. External triggers are also those text messages you get from fellow members bugging you to come to the next ride.

Internal triggers are more subtle but also more powerful. Internal triggers are urges and desires that push us to do something. The feeling of being tired may trigger you to buy a third cup of coffee. When you're hungry, you grab a snack. Stress from work may trigger you to check Twitter.

Internal triggers for Pinterest users may be boredom. Or it could be inspiration. They feel the need to be creative, so they pull up Pinterest to search for ideas. They curate their boards to reflect their ever-changing tastes and moods. The more often someone uses Pinterest to explore their creativity, the stronger that trigger becomes.

ACTION

If done right, your mix of internal and external triggers will encourage members to take your core action. Again, you need to be clear about what your single most important action is. People are busy, so if your members only did one thing to get the most out of your community, what would it be?

Your core action should be simple, stimulating, and meaningful. Ideally, it becomes a ritual. Fitness communities like SoulCycle, Peloton, and CrossFit imbue their classes with meaning. You aren't just working out; you're *overcoming* obstacles and *becoming* your best self. There's a reason why so many members refer to these classes as "going to church."

Your core action should be obsessively consistent, but the rewards should be variable.

REWARD

People don't just join communities for their own sake. They expect a meaningful reward for their time, money, and energy.

Yelp built their platform and community around a single core action: leave a review. They knew the top 1 percent of users left the majority of reviews on the site, so they tailored the rewards to appeal to their top users. Yelp gives out badges for different accomplishments, such as reviewing multiple brunch spots (The Breakfast Club badge) and reviewing restaurants in more than one state (The Statesman). But the ultimate reward for Yelpers is to become a member of the Yelp Elite Squad (YES!). This distinction earns you the coveted Elite badge and access to exclusive events.

Now here's the often-overlooked key to building a sticky experience: the reward can't be guaranteed every time. You need to keep members on their toes. *Variable rewards* are given out intermittently (i.e., every so often, not on a set schedule), which is much more exciting and sticky than rewards we come to expect. With variable rewards, people are more likely to continue taking the core action until they get rewarded again. Slot machines and casinos exploit this psychological quirk to make money. You can use it to hook members on positive community experiences.

On Yelp, Elite status is rewarded on a yearly basis, which means Yelpers need to earn it every year. It's never guaranteed they will get it again—they need to keep pace with the other top reviewers in their city. The uncertainty of earning Elite status makes the reward sweeter every time.

Variable rewards make your communities exciting and keep people coming back for more.

INVESTMENT

The last step of the Hook framework is investment. When someone takes an action and gets rewarded, they'll invest more time, money, or energy back into the community in hopes of another reward.

Sarah Tavel gave an excellent keynote at Traction Conf 2016. In that presentation, Tavel identified two types of investment: accruing benefits and mounting losses. Both are powerful tools for keeping members engaged.

Accruing benefits occur when a community, product, or service gets *better* the more you use it. Pinterest, for example, learns your likes and dislikes, and uses that data to curate your browsing experience. Other users can also follow your profile over time, which is a big benefit if you're trying to grow your personal or business brand. In communities like Startup Grind, Atlassian, or social sports leagues, accruing benefits come in the form of friendships and colleagues. Every event you attend where you meet someone new makes the next event better. Soon, you're not walking into a room full of strangers, but friends.

Mounting loss makes it more difficult to walk away from a community, product, or service the more you use it. If a user stops posting on Instagram or Twitter, they risk losing followers and engagement. Additionally, if a user does not actively engage with the content of others, they may feel like they are missing out on the latest trends, events, or news in their social circle. This fear of missing out can be a powerful motivator for users to continue using the platform and stay engaged with the content and connections they value. The more friends you have in a community, the smaller your social circle will be if you stop showing up. Peloton and other fitness communities use the psychology of mounting losses to keep us coming back every day. Peloton keeps track of your "streaks," or the number of consecutive days you ride. The longer your streak gets, the more you have to "lose" by not showing up. This is the same tactic Duolingo uses to keep you on track with your language lessons: show up every day, and don't break the streak.

Investment can also mean a literal investment in your community. Take Harley-Davidson, for example. HOG members spend on average 30 percent more on Harley merchandise than non-HOG members. This not only signals a monetary investment in the Harley brand, but an identity investment too. This is another example of mounting losses—the more someone identifies with Harley, the more they have to lose if they choose to leave their HOG.

Use Nir Eyal's Hook framework to map out your virtuous loop. Build it around your core action and make sure you vary up the rewards enough to keep people coming back for more. The tighter your virtuous loop, the more members will invest their time, money, energy, and *identity* in your community.

SHOW UP CONSISTENTLY

Consistency is the key ingredient for building a sticky community. You use consistent triggers to consistently drive your core action to consistently add value to your members' lives. Justin Vogel has held Safary community calls every Tuesday for over a year. Many HOG chapters host group rides on the same day each month. Consistency is how you turn an activity into a ritual, but of course, this takes time.

Many community leaders quit before they comprehend the benefits of consistency. It's a shame because you can do *everything* right in building your community, but if you're inconsistent, none of it will matter.

If you do nothing else, just keep showing up.

RULE 12:

"BE THAT PERSON
FOR YOUR
COMMUNITY, AND
THEY'LL REWARD
YOU WITH TRUST
AND SUPPORT
OF THEIR OWN."

TODAY, SAASTR IS known for its massive business "festivals" and for being the world's largest community for business software.

But rewind the clock ten years and you'll see none of the crowds or the hype. All you'll see is Jason Lemkin feverishly typing on his computer.

Before founding SaaStr, Jason started and sold a SaaS company called EchoSign. But instead of retiring early, he decided to share his lessons and insights with other SaaS founders. He did this primarily through Quora, the online Q&A platform. But Jason was no casual user; he posted twice a day, every day, for years. Through his efforts he grew a following on the platform, which then followed him to Twitter and LinkedIn. When he finally launched the SaaStr blog in 2012, he had a small audience ready to check out anything he created.

Jason continued his writing streak with the blog, crafting in-depth articles every week while still posting daily on Quora. He wrote about user activation rates, hiring sales execs, building software, finding co-founders, and every other topic that haunted SaaS founders. Word spread about Jason and his blog, and over the next three years, his audience grew exponentially. The active comments section bred helpful (and sometimes heated) discussions about the right and wrong way to do things. Through these interactions, founders made connections with other members of Jason's audience. They helped each other, rooted for each other, and even began to work together. SaaStr no longer had just an audience— it was growing a community.

In 2013, Jason held the first SaaStr Social in Menlo Park, California. The space only had room for a few hundred people, but it was an instant hit with those who showed up. The SaaStr community continued to grow—online and off—for another two years. In 2015, Jason hosted the first SaaStr Conference, and the rest is history.

Since then, SaaStr has expanded globally, hosting an annual SaaStr Conference in Europe since 2018 and launching the first SaaStr APAC (Asia-Pacific) in 2023. More than 100,000 people attend live SaaStr events every year, and it's widely regarded as the gold standard of tech events.

Seeing SaaStr today, you'd never expect it to have such humble beginnings. Jason's story is testament to the power of small, consistent actions when building your community.

CONSISTENCY IS A RARE COMMODITY

The world seems to become more unpredictable by the day. Trusted leaders and institutions go back on their word at the first whiff of opportunity. Politicians fail to make good on the promises that got them elected. Large companies lay off employees by the thousands as soon as times get tough. The only thing that's consistent about these times is *inconsistency*.

But consistency is something we all need. We crave it as children as we try to make sense of this hectic world, and we crave it as adults when we learn the world will never make sense. So when a person finds a source of consistency—something they can count on, day in and day out—they latch on to it. Not only is consistency key to building sticky communities, but it's also the foundation of any trusting relationship.

So if consistency is so important, why do so many community leaders fail to deliver it? Simply put, consistency is *hard*. It requires patience, doggedness, and long-term thinking in the face of months, even years of unimpressive results. But that's the type of commitment it takes to build a Harley-Davidson, an Atlassian, or a SaaStr. Communities are built one brick at a time.

Here's the good news: The benefits of consistent action don't grow linearly. They go exponential.

Like compounding interest, you'll hardly notice the impact of consistent action at first. But then, seemingly overnight, things will change. You won't just add a few more members each week, you'll double in size. Then you'll double again. Suddenly, everyone in your industry is talking about you and knocking on your door to get into the club. It will be like someone finally switched on the lights. All those thankless days and nights you spent in the early days? You were simply building the potential energy needed to explode.

But the opposite is true too. Skip a week—even a day—and the magic of compounding interest works against you. Your members won't wait around for you to come back at your convenience. As soon as you break your consistency, you begin to break their trust. They'll quickly be on the hunt for a better place to spend their time. You could nail every other strategy I share in this book, but without consistency, your community will crumble.

That doesn't mean you need to be a superhuman with the grit of Captain America. You don't need to spend every waking moment building your community. Your life outside work doesn't need to suffer.

The key to long-term consistency is *sustainable* consistency. And the key to sustainable consistency is building systems.

BUILDING A SYSTEM FOR CONSISTENT ACTION

James Clear wrote in his book *Atomic Habits*: "You do not rise to the level of your goals. You fall to the level of your systems."

A system is a collection of tools, processes, and daily habits that help you deliver a consistent result. Without a system to manage your community, your actions will ebb and flow dramatically based on your schedule and even your mood. Humans can't always be their absolute best, but with the right system, your community can.

It took me years to build the right system that helped me run Traction consistently. Before that, I ran it on sheer determination, waking up in the middle of the night to create content if I failed to get it done the day before. I refused to break the trust of my fledgling community, but my work pattern was unsustainable. I needed to figure out how to do the work with less effort.

The system my team and I created is simple. Some would call it unsophisticated, but that just makes it repeatable. Repeatable tasks are your best friend when building a community. Consistency requires simplicity.

Here's how we developed our system for running Traction:

+ Focus on Your Core Action
+ Use Checklists for Everything
+ Create a Member Database
+ Get Personal . . . at Scale
+ Keep Your Calendar Full
+ Quantity over Quality
+ Accept Accountability

FOCUS ON YOUR CORE ACTION

In his book, *The One Thing*, founder Gary Keller of Keller Williams Realty shares his simple approach to success: "When you want the absolute best chance to succeed at anything you want, your approach should always be the same. Go small."

By "small," Keller didn't mean insignificant. Just the opposite. If you want to build something meaningful, you must focus on the *single most significant* thing and ignore the rest. In other words, focus on your *core action*. As we talked about in Rule 11, a core action is the event or activity that anchors the member experience. It's the *one thing* every member participates in. Done consistently enough, your core action becomes a beloved ritual.

Your system must be built around your core action and keep it happening on schedule. Whether it's a daily LinkedIn post, weekly podcast, monthly event, or annual conference, everything you do should be in service of consistently delivering your core action.

But what if you don't have the means to deliver on your core action right away? What if you want to build the largest in-person event in your industry, but all you have is a Twitter account and free Discord channel? If you're as impatient as I am, you'll want to jump straight to the grand vision. But it doesn't work like that. Your core action must be something you can deliver consistently *today*. Scale down your aspirations (for now) and start building where you are. Over time, your core action can evolve along with your community. Jason Lemkin's original core action was posting on Quora twice a day. When his Quora audience got large enough, he started publishing blog posts. After three years of blogging, he finally had the means to launch an in-person conference. A few years after that, he got his roving robot dance floor.

Growing anything—whether it's a community, a business, or a nonprofit organization—is hard enough on its own. Don't overcomplicate it by diluting your attention. Focus on a single core action you can take *today* and build a system to deliver on it.

USE CHECKLISTS FOR EVERYTHING

What should that system look like? Again, I prefer to keep it simple. And there's no tool more simple (and in my opinion, more powerful), than the humble checklist.

Dr. Atul Gawande has done extensive research on the power of checklists, which he shares in his book, *The Checklist Manifesto*. Checklists improve results in virtually every profession, even those with life-and-death implications. Adopting checklists in hospital operating rooms resulted in fewer malpractice incidents caused by doctors or nurses forgetting to do something routine. Airline pilots use checklists to reduce the risk of missing a critical takeoff or landing step. If checklists work in these high-stakes environments, they will surely work for your community, like they have in mine.

We've recorded two online webinars every week for almost three years. This is in addition to our annual conference, which is a year-long planning effort. The key to our success is a checklist for every event. Our webinar checklist lives in a Google spreadsheet, and it helps me track every step we need to take: invite potential guests, confirm guests, schedule the call, send a confirmation email, research upcoming guests, prepare questions, promote on LinkedIn and via email, host the webinar, publish on YouTube, and create social media content.

But the checklist doesn't end there. I also sync up each task with my calendar so I have a scheduled block of time to complete it. This technique, called time-blocking, is an absolute game-changer. I set up recurring calendar events for every repeatable task so that I *know* I'll have time to do them. This makes things easy; when my calendar says it's time to do something, I do it.

My checklist and calendar system allows me to manage up to ten upcoming webinars at once without missing a step. If you do something more than once, build a checklist for it. When things start to get hectic, you'll be glad you did.

CREATE A MEMBER DATABASE

Communication is the cornerstone of every community. But blindly blasting your email list is not an effective way to connect with people. The more you know about each individual member, the better you can tailor your message to them.

This is why you need a member database.

In sales, companies use customer relationship management systems (CRMs) to capture key information about potential customers and track their ongoing conversations with them. Salesforce is the most popular CRM in the world, and it allows salespeople to track everything from job title to favorite pizza toppings. Salespeople use CRMs to take notes after each conversation, so each touch point feels like it's building on the last one.

As a community leader, you don't need a tool as complex as Salesforce. You can build a usable CRM right in a spreadsheet. Or you can use your email subscription tool to track information about your members. I'll hold off on making specific tool recommendations since they change constantly. But whether you use a Rolodex or some futuristic AI-powered tool, you're going to need a member database.

Important information to track for each member:

+ Name (obviously)
+ Email address
+ Job title
+ Place of employment
+ Mailing address (to send gifts, swag, and physical invitations)
+ Birthday (to give you a reason to send gifts)
+ Email open rates
+ Clickthrough rates
+ Event registrations
+ Event attendance
+ Volunteer history
+ Any other touch points members have with the community

Most of this information is standard in any CRM. The only manual information you'll want to track is live event attendance and volunteer history; this will help you identify and reward your champions (see Rule 10).

Having an up-to-date CRM gives you enormous leverage, especially when it comes to member outreach. The more information you have, the more personalized you can make your communication.

GET PERSONAL . . . AT SCALE

Personalized communication is the difference between building a community and building an audience. If everyone in your community gets the exact same message, you're not actually engaging; you're just broadcasting. And when you broadcast, people tune out.

You probably have an email marketing tool already, but chances are you're not using it to its fullest capability. If you're just collecting emails and sending out the occasional newsletter, you're missing an opportunity to build deeper relationships with your members.

When you combine your CRM and email marketing platform, magic happens. These tools allow you to deliver personalized communication *at scale*.

The simplest way to personalize an email is to address your member by name. Most email marketing tools allow you to do this. They call the feature "Personalization" or "Mail Merge." Using someone's name will always grab their attention, even in a crowded email inbox.

But there's so much more you can do. Remember those engagement stats we told you to track in your CRM?

You can also use those to tag certain members for unique emails. Imagine sending a special opportunity only to those members who have volunteered in the last twelve months. That's how you turn eager contributors into superfans. On the other end of the spectrum, you can send re-engagement emails to members who have been inactive for six months. This is a friendly nudge, saying "We miss you! Want to join our next event?" Sometimes, that's all it takes to restart the relationship.

Email marketing and CRM tools have been around for decades, but I still see many community leaders failing to use them properly (or at all). They fall into one of two camps: either they believe personalized communication can *only* be done one message at a time, or they believe personal messages are no longer important. Both parties are wrong. With more community options than ever before, people will flock to those that *consistently* deliver a *personalized* experience. The bar has been raised for all of us.

Luckily, these tools are just getting better. Now you can automatically personalize full passages in your email depending on the engagement level of your members. That means your oldest, most engaged members will receive a different message than your newest members. How awesome is that? Some email marketing tools now come with built-in recommendation systems as well. That means your members can invite their friends to join with just one click.

As your community grows, member outreach will take up a disproportionate amount of your time. Eventually, you won't be able to keep up with it all. Before you get to that point, build a system that lets you deliver *personalized* communication . . . *at scale.*

KEEP YOUR CALENDAR FULL

The early days of community-building are a slog. It's a ton of work, and very few people will notice. It doesn't feel as rewarding as you expect. Your community-market fit isn't quite right, and growth is hard. This is the moment where most people quit, and their dreams of building a community fade away.

But you can avoid this fate. The best way to keep going when things get hard is to keep your calendar full. "In the more than ten years I've been interviewing, I've rarely had a month without at least five guests booked in advance," said Andrew Warner, host of the *Mixergy Startup Stories* podcast and author of *Stop Asking Questions.* "That's how I keep getting past my inner doubt and continue improving."

Fill up your calendar during optimistic times to keep you going during down times. If you commit to hosting one webinar per week, schedule guests four to six weeks out. When you have a particularly rough week, the kind that makes you want to quit, you won't be able to. Because your next event is already on the books.

Keeping your calendar full will also help you focus on the things within your control: showing up every day, week, and month to deliver a great community experience. You don't have full say over how many people join your group, but you can control how many times you post on your forum each week, or how many meetups you schedule each month.

Your community will live and die by the calendar. Keep it full to keep up the momentum.

QUANTITY OVER QUALITY

To establish a consistent habit, it is more important to focus on the quantity of the work being done rather than the quality of the work. Build momentum and create a routine that eventually becomes a habit, which can then be refined and improved over time.

At age forty-two, I'm currently in the best shape of my life. I've lost over fifty pounds in the last year, but it's not because I eat perfectly and lift like an Olympian. Two small habits have driven my transformation: intermittent fasting and daily push-ups to start my day. These are not the only things I do—I also cut out processed food, hired a personal trainer, and lift weights four to five times a week—but these tiny habits built the foundation for my healthy lifestyle. I would not have kept up with the bigger wellness activities without my small, daily routines.

Never underestimate the power of small actions taken consistently over time.

What does quality over quantity mean for building your community? It means starting conversations in your online chat group every day. It means hosting a weekly webinar no matter what. It means planning in-person meetups every other week like clockwork. It means replying to every comment left by another member without exception. Find one small thing—anything—to do every day. This is how you build the foundation of high-quality habits.

Too many people wait to take action until they're "good enough." This is the biggest fallacy in life. Taking action is the prerequisite to good enough work. If you never start, you'll never get there.

LAST THING: ACCEPT ACCOUNTABILITY

Consistency is a rare commodity because it's hard to pull off. Anyone can start something, but few keep it going day after day, years on end. If you can be one of those people, you'll be rewarded with a passionate community of raving fans.

The steps in this rule have helped me deliver consistently for almost ten years. But there's one more element that you'll need, and that's the human element. Don't attempt to build your community on your own, in the dark. Tell people what you're doing, what your goals are, and what they should expect from you. Use other people's expectations as fuel to stick to your word and stay consistent. This is what it means to be accountable.

One of the best ways to be accountable is to build your community in public. Share your progress each step of the way—your wins, losses, and lessons learned. But no matter what, just show up. Each time you deliver on your promise, you'll feel more comfortable with accountability, and you'll start to build the habit of consistency. Building in public is also a fantastic growth strategy. By documenting your journey, you'll attract early supporters who believe in what you're doing.

Accountability is the difference between professionals and amateurs. Professionals accept accountability with open arms. They know that by taking responsibility, they will be rewarded with trust. Amateurs fear accountability because they don't trust themselves to deliver. And if you don't trust yourself, don't expect others to trust you either. If you're not as consistent as you want to be, focus on becoming accountable instead.

Remember, community-led growth is not a marketing tactic. It's all about people. In your life, you trust those who show up for you consistently. Be *that* person for your community members, and they'll reward you with trust and support of their own.

BONUS CONTENT

Get more community-led growth tools, resources, and case studies by going to:

WWW.LLOYEDLOBO.COM/BONUS

RULE 13:

MEASURE AND MONETIZE

"IT'S NOT ABOUT THE METRICS. IT'S ABOUT ASKING THE RIGHT QUESTIONS."

THE ROOM WAS packed, but I could see his expression across the sea of faces. He wasn't happy. I headed over to him after the event, making my way through the dispersing crowd and stepping over piles of pizza boxes. The owner of the coworking space was standing with his arms crossed, waiting. "You broke fire code tonight," he said.

Traction had officially outgrown its first home.

It was a big day for our community. It meant it was time for us to grow up. I had never taken an official headcount at our meetups, but now we'd need to find a real event space and take our planning more seriously. This would cost money, which meant it was also time to monetize. But how could we monetize if I didn't even know how many people were at our events?

Communities can only last so long without a process for measuring their impact. Eventually, the people funding you—whether it's a parent company/brand, sponsors, or paying members—will demand to see some numbers. At the very least, you should know how many people are showing up so you don't break fire code. Lesson learned.

The challenge is that community growth—and community-*led* growth—will always be part art and part science. Success comes from a mix of sources, touch points, content, and experiences. In the marketing world, this is called "multi-touch attribution," and companies like Google and Meta spend billions trying to accurately measure it. If they still struggle, it's ok to expect you might too.

At Boast.AI, we always knew that Traction was our biggest growth channel, but we couldn't measure it the way we could measure sales or programmatic marketing. Gainsight has had the same challenge. "Our own conference [Pulse] is the most important thing we've ever done, but it's also the least measurable," said Gainsight founder, Nick Mehta, at Traction Conf 2019.

But the fact that community is difficult to measure won't make your sponsors or CFO feel any better. In lean times, the least effective programs get cut. If you can't make a data-driven case for your community, best believe you'll be at the top of that list. So how do we measure the effectiveness of our community efforts?

It's easy to get lost in the alphabet soup of metrics like ROAS and ARPU. It gives even an engineer like me a migraine. Instead, I prefer thinking through the most fundamental questions I need to answer about member growth:

- Do they show up?
- Do they pay?
- Do they stay?
- Do they bring their friends?
- How much does it cost?

You don't need to perfectly measure attribution or your community's exact ROI on your business. Instead, these five questions will give you an accurate and useful snapshot of how you're performing.

Let's dig into each question and identify some useful metrics for answering them.

STAGE	QUESTION	KEY METRICS	CURRENT RATES	TARGET RATES
ACQUISITION	Do they show up?	Open and click through rates, Events RSVPs		
RETENTION	Do they stay?	NRR, churn rate, DAU, WAU		
REFERRAL	Do they bring their friends?	NPS, referrals per member		
REVENUE	Do they pay?	Ticket sales, premium users, sponsorships		
PROFITABILITY	Does it make money?	Net profit = Total Revenue –Total Expenses		

Inspired by Pirate Metrics from 500 Startups

DO THEY SHOW UP?

The first question you need to answer is the simplest one. Are people showing up at your events, in your group, or on your webinars? Are they opening your emails, accepting your invitations, and signing up for activities? And how are these numbers changing over time?

This question represents the top-line growth for your community. The target metric will be different depending on the type of programming you run.

Popular answers (aka, metrics) to this question include:

+ Number of email subscribers
+ Open and clickthrough rates
+ Event RSVPs and attendance (online or in-person)
+ Number of repeat RSVPs
+ New sign ups

+ Number of reviews/comments/questions left (in
  the case of forums or review sites)

This is the easiest and most basic question to answer about growth. Most communities have *some* idea of how many people are showing up. But it's a misleading indicator on its own. Like we saw in Rule 11: Make Your Community Sticky, many communities suffer from empty-calories growth. They lose members just as fast as they get them, if not faster. This is not sustainable.

"Do they show up?" is a great place to start measuring the impact of your community, but answer the next four questions to round out the picture.

DO THEY PAY?

Some community builders bristle at the topic of monetization. Please hear me out before calling me a greedy capitalist and throwing this book away. Even if your community is free, you still need a monetization strategy to be sustainable for the long-term.

In short, nothing in life is free, especially building and maintaining a community. No community in history—and I'm talking all the way back to the first human settlements—has survived without providing for itself. If you aren't making money directly from your members or sponsors, you better be generating revenue for your parent company. If you're not doing that, you need to attract donors and grants. If you're not doing *that*, you need to have the funds to support yourself as you build. If you have none of these things, it will be difficult to keep going for long.

The best communities give away tons of free value before monetizing. But they *do* eventually monetize. There are many ways to generate revenue: charge membership fees like Harley Owners Groups, the Freemasons, and professional groups like Pavilion, a community for Revenue Operations leaders; earn money from advertising like Yelp, or sponsorships like Physician Moms Group; upsell members on paid products or services like CPOHQ, which drives business for its parent company, Knoetic; run premium events and experiences like Startup Grind and Traction. The most sustainable communities are built on several of these revenue channels.

Here is an incomplete list of monetization channels for your community:

+ Memberships (Pavilion)

+ Events (SaaStr, Traction)

+ Products and Services (CPOHQ, Red Bull)

+ Courses and Education (Duolingo)

+ Sponsorships (Physician Moms Group)

+ Advertising (Yelp)

+ Platform Ad Revenue (YouTube or TikTok influencers)

+ Premium Content (Patreon users, Duolingo Premium)

+ Donations and Grants (nonprofits)

Another example comes from Nas Daily. In addition to the Nas Creator Accelerator course, Nuseir Yassin's company hosts creator summits around the world. Members pay to attend and sponsors like YouTube and Meta pay for exposure. Nas also works directly with major brands through Nas Studios, and he recently launched a SaaS platform for communities called Nas.io. This is all on top of the money he earns from his "free" content on YouTube, TikTok, and other social media channels.

If you're dead set on running a free community, at least consider a premium tier of membership for your champions and superfans. Paying members will get the elevated experience they want while subsidizing the community for everyone else. It's a win-win.

The more monetization channels you can spin up, the most sustainable your community will be for the long term.

DO THEY STAY?

Making money off a one-time event is a great start, but it's not sustainable. If none of those attendees come back for future events, you might be falling into the empty-calories growth trap.

The question "Do they stay?" refers to the all-important measurement of *retention*. Can you keep people coming back week after week, year after year?

Retention is just as important as your top-line growth. A study conducted by Bain & Company and Harvard Business School found that increasing customer retention by 5 percent can increase profits by 25–95 percent. This phenomenon can be tracked with a metric called Net Revenue Retention (NRR), or how much revenue is generated from existing customers over a set period. World-class companies and communities have an NRR of greater than 100 percent, meaning their revenue is increasing faster than their customer base. If you have a strong NRR, you could go without ever adding a new customer and *still* grow your bottom line.

Here's how NRR works: Say your business enters January with a monthly recurring revenue (MRR) of $27,000. Your company upgrades two subscriptions of existing customers worth $4,000 each, raising your MRR to $35,000. Later in the month, you lose $5,000 in revenue churn due to contract expirations. Your net revenue retention for January is 111 percent ($30,000 ÷ $27,000).

A competitor enters January with an MRR of $40,000. Two customers downgrade their subscription by $2,000 each. There are no customers upgrades. Their net revenue retention for January is 90 percent ($36,000 ÷ $40,000).

NRR isn't the only retention-focused metric to track. Daily Active Users (DAU) and Weekly Active Users (WAU) are both valuable depending on the type of community you're building. Joseph Quan of CPOHQ started out tracking WAUs. His hypothesis, when starting a community for Chief People Officers, was that their best users would return on a weekly basis. As CPOHQ grew, so did the value it provided to its members, and Quan transitioned to tracking DAUs as well. Both DAUs and WAUs are great metrics for online communities.

If you're running regular live events, like Traction's webinars, another valuable metric is percentage of return members. How many people have shown up to multiple events? If each event is 100 percent new people, that's a sign you're not creating enough value for people to return.

Popular metrics to track for this question:

+ Net Revenue Retention (NRR)

+ Churn (opposite of retention rate)

+ Daily Active Users

+ Weekly Active Users

+ Returning Users

+ Average Viewing Time (for video or webinars)

+ Average Session Duration (for web pages or forums)

Asking the retention question will also help you identify your superfans: the members who stay for months, even years on end, and who always show up to the next event.

DO THEY BRING THEIR FRIENDS?

There are many ways to grow your community, but the absolute most effective way is word of mouth, or WoM. WoM is free and by far the most convincing form of marketing in the universe. If you can harness it, your community will be unstoppable.

Word of mouth has always been difficult to measure because it often happens one-on-one between friends and colleagues. One tried-and-true approach to tracking WoM is to survey new members, "How did you hear about us?" This will paint an incomplete picture, but it's better than nothing.

Another imperfect metric is the Net Promoter Score, or NPS. NPS is a popular tool that measures the likelihood of members inviting their friends. But it doesn't tell you if, when, or how many friends they actually do invite.

AnyRoad, the experiential marketing platform, takes NPS to a new level by tracking it before *and* after a specific event. Before an event begins, AnyRoad helps its clients survey attendees: "How likely are you to recommend [brand or community] to a friend?" NPS is always measured on a scale of 1–10. Scores of 9 or 10 indicate a brand promoter, 7–8 are neutral, and any score 6 or less is considered a detractor. After the event, AnyRoad will survey attendees again and then measure the delta between the two datasets. In other words, did the event convert attendees into brand promoters? If you have the means, I recommend trying this approach.

One of the most effective ways to answer this question is to set up a referral program. Referral programs are incredibly powerful, and they are a way of rewarding your biggest fans. It will cost you money—either in the form of direct payouts or other gifts for referrers, plus discounts to referred new members—but it's essentially free money. You only pay when you get a new member, so it's a pretty good deal. Many software tools exist to help you set up a referral program. I highly recommend it.

Metrics to answer this question:

+ Net Promoter Score
+ Total referrals (identify your top referrers and shower them with rewards and recognition; see Rule 10)
+ Referrals per member
+ Survey question: "How did you hear about us?"

When it comes to word of mouth, don't let perfect be the enemy of *good enough*. Find your members who invite the most people and incentivize them to do it more.

DOES IT MAKE MONEY?

You can start a community for virtually nothing. But as you grow, your expenses will too. This is what happened to Traction when we outgrew our coworking space. We weren't just paying for pizza and drinks anymore; we had venue rentals, security, insurance, and other costs to track. Managing finances can become a full-time job in itself, but it's absolutely critical to know what you're spending on.

FIXED COSTS: Some expenses will basically stay the same no matter what you do or how many members you have. These include many technology costs like your website, CRM (though pricing goes up the more contacts you have), email (same as CRM), marketing automation, and communication tools like Zoom. As your community grows, you'll add more fixed costs such as staff salaries and possibly rent.

Consider your fixed costs as your "keeping the lights on" expenses. This is the bare minimum you need to cover.

PROGRAMMING AND CONTENT COSTS: The money you spend on events, content, and other programming are variable costs. These expenses include venue fees, speaker fees and travel, catering, design (both physical like exhibits, booths, and posters as well as digital), audio visual services, travel and hotel for staff, security, insurance, and gifts for speakers and volunteers. You may also pay content creators, course managers, and social media coordinators for your digital programming.

Programming costs can get out of hand quickly. This is where many communities run into trouble. Below I'll share a breakdown of expenses to look out for.

TALENT FEES: Speakers and performers vary in cost, from free to millions of dollars. It's not about getting the most expensive talent, but finding the *right* talent for your event. No matter the speaking or performance fees, you'll want to budget in other expenses as well, such as travel, accommodations, and food.

VENUE COSTS: The cost of the venue is one of the largest line items for any event. Not only are you paying for the space, but there are always significant upcharges that are not explicitly stated in the quote. Look for add-on expenses like rental fees, catering, security, insurance, and on-site medical staff. Outdoor events come with their own sets of costs, including tents, heaters, tables and seating, and holding a backup venue in case you get rained out.

TICKETING FEES: Most events will require the use of a ticket platform that will charge a percentage-based ticketing fee along with a payment processing fee. Watch these fees up front as they can balloon and eat into your profit. The best way to overcome this is to pass these fees on to the ticket buyer.

MARKETING AND PROMOTION: Paid promotion is a delicate balancing act. Spend too much and you'll struggle to break even. Spend too little and you won't fill enough seats. I believe the best marketing is free—word-of-mouth, email, and content—but even free marketing comes at a price. Who is creating your content and managing your email list? If you're relying on word-of-mouth, consider setting up a referral program. This will incentivize your biggest fans to invite their friends and colleagues, but this will also eat into your profit.

VOLUNTEERS: Many first-time community leaders make the mistake of thinking volunteers are free labor. This is *not* true. Volunteers may not be paid, but they still expect some type of compensation. This could include free meals, gifts, training, and event-branded clothing. Make sure you keep a volunteer line item in your budget.

ASK THE *RIGHT* QUESTIONS

You will never be able to measure the ROI of your community perfectly. Humans are too messy and unpredictable for such precision. But that's ok, because you can still get an accurate picture with the five questions described in this rule:

+ Do they show up?
+ Do they pay?
+ Do they stay?
+ Do they bring their friends?
+ Does it make money?

Measuring the health and growth of your community is not about the metrics. It's about asking the right questions, then finding the right answers. Identify the metrics that work best to answer each question. Then track them religiously. Next time you need answers on the effectiveness of your community, you'll have the data ready to go. And if all goes well, those numbers will keep going up and to the right.

THIS IS
THE SIGN
YOU'VE BEEN
LOOKING FOR

CONCLUSION:

BUILD A COMMUNITY, CHANGE THE WORLD

" COMMUNITY ISN'T JUST A PLACE, BUT A FEELING. BUILD IT WHEREVER YOU GO, AND YOU'LL NEVER BE ALONE. "

WHEN I FIRST invited founders to my Calgary coworking space for pizza and networking, I had no idea it would fundamentally change the way I thought about business.

But as those meetups grew and the group of strangers I assembled became friends and colleagues, it dawned on me: I had experienced this feeling before. Way back before I became an entrepreneur, and even before I moved to North America. It was the same feeling I had during those fateful days of the Persian Gulf War, living in danger but surrounded by a community that would do anything for each other. It felt like home. It also felt like the future.

The way we do business must fundamentally change. Traditional marketing has become more expensive and less effective. The brand authenticity movement has turned every company into a snarky thirteen-year-old with a Twitter account. Customer satisfaction is at an all-time low while corporate profits soar. We're so focused on B2B and B2C and B2B2C that we forget business is always P2P—people-to-people.

But I have hope.

Every day, consumers around the world are realizing they don't just want products or services. They need *meaning* in their lives. They want to experience connection, autonomy, mastery, purpose, energy, and recognition. And when they find it, they're hooked for life. This is why the earliest community-led companies succeeded so wildly: Harley-Davidson, Apple, Red Bull, and others. Newer companies like HubSpot, Sales Hacker,

Startup Grind, Knoetic, Yelp, Duolingo, and Boast.AI followed this legacy.

Who will build the next great community-led company? I hope, after reading this book, the answer is *you*.

Community-led growth is not a new concept, but today, it's more important than ever. With more choices at their disposal, customers are choosing brands that make them feel at home. Brands that don't just provide goods and services, but experiences, friendships, and personal growth. And people aren't just spending money on vacations and restaurants anymore, but standalone communities that surround them with *their* people, and those they aspire to be.

But community-building goes beyond commerce. There is extensive research on how strong social connections are linked to reduced anxiety and depression, higher self-esteem, and increased empathy, trust, and cooperation. On the other hand, a lack of social connections can cause a decline in physical and mental health and overall worse well being.

My goal with this book is to show you why community-led growth is the future of business and a net positive for the world. If you're brand-new to community-building, use this book as a roadmap to get you started and avoid many of the pitfalls I experienced personally. If you're a seasoned community leader, I hope I inspired you with new ideas and insights. At the very least, I hope you're more bullish on community than ever before. I certainly am.

Now it's time to put the lessons of this book into action. If you're not sure where to start, here's what I recommend.

First, evaluate your community using the CAMPER model. On a scale of 1–5, rate how well your community is delivering each principle: connection, autonomy, mastery, purpose, energy, and recognition. Better yet, ask your community members to fill out this survey for you. Make sure it's anonymous and be prepared for difficult feedback.

If you haven't started building your community yet, first determine what type of community you want to build. Is it a community of practice, product, play, or a combination of them? In other words, what do you want your members to get out of their community experience? This is the first and most crucial question for building a strong community. If you have already started your group, make sure you're clear on the type of experience you're trying to deliver.

Continue going through each Rule in this book, building your community plan step by step: discover your Why, set an inspiring goal, choose one audience to serve exceptionally well, then nail the community experience before attempting to scale it. Wow community members from day one by crafting an "Aha" Moment, then turn your events into multisensory wonderlands. Don't forget to involve your community every step of the way and reward your champions with recognition and opportunities for growth. Build on your early success by engineering virtuous loops that make your community sticky.

If you do all this consistently for months, even years on end, you will win. Finally, be sure to measure what matters and *monetize* so you can build a healthy, sustainable community.

Community-led growth is simple, but far from easy. If you don't love serving people and making them feel included, it will be hard to succeed. Community is a long game, and there will be times when results are slow and the effort doesn't seem worth it. Every community builder experiences times like this. The difference with successful community leaders is that they keep going where others quit.

If you believe in the power of community-led growth but don't have the time or inclination to do it yourself, I recommend hiring a passionate community builder to lead your efforts. Many companies are heading this direction, as evidenced by the growing job listings for Head of Community. You can now find community leaders with a decade or more of experience. Whatever salary you pay them will be well worth it in the long run.

I'll leave you with this: whatever you do next after reading this book, I hope it's something that brings you joy and energy. Life is too short to spend on things you don't love or with people you don't like. Community isn't just a place, but a feeling. Build it wherever you go, and you'll never be alone.

ACKNOWLEDGMENTS

I WOULD NOT BE the person I am today without my community of family, friends, colleagues, and mentors.

I would like to express my deepest gratitude to my parents—Elsie and Louis—and my sister, Loraine, for their unwavering support and guidance. Together, we experienced the profound impact of community during the Gulf War, a time that taught us the power of solidarity and compassion. Mom and Dad, thanks for instilling in me the essence of community building and teaching me that true abundance in life can only be created by selflessly helping others, without any expectations of help in return. Your teachings have been the cornerstone of my values and have shaped my perspective on the world.

A special appreciation goes to my grandparents, who emerged from extreme poverty in India. Despite their difficult circumstances, they exemplified boundless generosity and hospitality, always welcoming strangers into their home with open arms. They instilled in me the belief that acts of kindness have a way of returning to us in unexpected ways, illustrating the inherent power of karma.

To my beloved wife, Viveta, and our precious children—Olivia, Emilia, and Zane—I am forever grateful. Vivi, your unending love and support have been the driving force behind my journey. You have been a constant source of strength, nourishing our family during the challenging times whenever I faced setbacks, of which there were many over the twenty-three years we've been together. When I lost sight of my identity after leaving the company I co-founded, you stood as a guiding light, leading me back toward the path of self-discovery. Your inspiration drives me to become the best version of myself.

I owe an immeasurable debt of gratitude to my first cousin, Sachin Brian Mendonca, whom I consider my real brother. You helped me discover my life's purpose, igniting within me the realization that I draw true happiness from bringing people together. Through life's toughest moments, your constant presence has been a source of solace and encouragement.

To Alex Popa, my co-founder at Boast.AI and Traction. From our initial days as partners in various university projects, to our enduring friendship and shared ventures to being neighbors in Dubai, it's been a rollercoaster ride. I will always be grateful to you for asking me to be your co-founder at Boast.AI. Thank you for your camaraderie through the highs and lows of our entrepreneurial journey.

To Ray Walia, my co-founder in Traction, I extend my sincere appreciation. Ray, you have been more than just a collaborator; you have been a true friend and an invaluable guide throughout our journey. Your advice and encouragement have consistently propelled me forward.

To Melissa Kwan, my dear friend, trusted confidant, and agony aunt. Thank you for being my voice of reason, never hesitating to offer tough love and shoot straight to help me see through the challenges I faced.

To Jason Lemkin, my esteemed mentor, motivator, inspiration, and guide, I am eternally grateful. When Boast.AI was a fledgling startup grappling with financial constraints, you gave us the incredible gift of free booths and access at SaaStr. Your responsiveness and thoughtfulness when I approached you to write the foreword for my book were truly heartwarming. Your willingness to always lend your voice and expertise without hesitation is a testament to your genuine commitment to supporting and uplifting others. Thank you for being an invaluable part of my journey.

Lastly, I would like to express my deepest appreciation to the Traction Community. Your collective wisdom, innovative spirit, and relentless commitment to progress have enriched my understanding in ways that surpass my ability to express. Together, let us continue to push the boundaries of innovation and create a transformative impact on the world.

SOURCES AND CITATIONS

Andersen, Derek. "Playbook for Building Communities, Superfans & Evangelists for Your Product." *Traction Conf.* September 17, 2019. https://www.youtube.com/watch?v=-5y54hANpe8.

Aragon, Kathryn. "3-Step Guide: How to Create Your Ideal Customer Profile (ICP)." *Sales Hacker.* March 28, 2023. https://www.saleshacker.com/ideal-customer-profile/.

Atlassian Community. "2021 Atlassian Community Year in Review." December 20, 2021. https://community.atlassian.com/t5/Watercooler-articles/2021-Atlassian-Community-Year-in-Review/ba-p/1886322.

Bharadwaj, Anu. "Building Connection in a Distributed World." *Traction Conf.* August 24, 2022. https://www.youtube.com/watch?v=aJQINMRJX0Y.

Bush, Wes. "How to Identify Your Product's Aha Moment." *ProductLed Blog.* October 5, 2022. https://productled.com/blog/how-to-identify-your-products-aha-moment/.

Computer History Museum. "The Homebrew Computer Club." https://www.computerhistory.org/revolution/personal-computers/17/312#:~:text=When%20Steve%20Jobs%20and%20Steve,a%20forum%20for%20sharing%20ideas.

Cuofano, Gennaro. "Virtuous Cycle: The Core Growth Model For Platforms." *FourWeekMBA.* February 5, 2023. https://fourweekmba.com/virtuous-cycle/.

Davidson, Willie G. *100 Years of Harley-Davidson.* New York: Bulfinch Press, 2002.

Dholakia, Utpal Ph.D. "3 Reasons Why Brand-Specific Rituals Are So Powerful." *Psychology Today*, March 22, 2016. https://www.psychologytoday.com/us/blog/the-science-behind-behavior/201603/3-reasons-why-brand-specific-rituals-are-so-powerful.

EQB Systems. "177: Lloyed Lobo Reveals How to Quickly Secure R&D Tax Credits for Funding Business Innovation with Boast.AI." *Business Infrastructure - Curing Back Office Blues*. https://www.eqbsystems.com/podcast/177-lloyd-lobo-reveals-how-to-quickly-secure-rd-tax-credits-for-funding-business-innovation-with-boast-ai.

Eyal, Nir. *Hooked*. 1st Edition. New York: Portfolio, 2014.

First Round. "A Founder's Step-by-Step Guide to Getting Your First 1,000 Community Members." https://firstround.com/review/a-founders-step-by-step-guide-to-getting-your-first-1000-community-members/.

First Round. "From Instant Pot to Instagram: Critical Lessons in Startup Community Building." https://review.firstround.com/from-instant-pot-to-instagram-critical-lessons-in-startup-community-building.

Fournier, Susan, and Lara Lee. "Getting Brand Communities Right." *Harvard Business Review*. April 2009. https://hbr.org/2009/04/getting-brand-communities-right.

Ghosh, Sudipto. "Salesforce Acquires The CMO Club to Unify Marketing Thoughts with B2B Practices." *MarTech Series*. March 3, 2020. https://martechseries.com/sales-marketing/crm/salesforce-acquires-the-cmo-club-to-unify-marketing-thoughts-with-b2b-practices/.

GitLab. "GitLab Heroes: Building GitLab together." https://about.gitlab.com/community/heroes/.

GitLab. "GitLab.com database incident." February 1, 2017. https://about.gitlab.com/blog/2017/02/01/gitlab-dot-com-database-incident/.

GitLab. "Postmortem of database outage of January 31." February 10, 2017. https://about.gitlab.com/blog/2017/02/10/postmortem-of-database-outage-of-january-31/.

Greene, Robert. *The 33 Strategies of War*. Reprint Edition. New York: Penguin Books, 2007.

Harvard Business Review. "The Science of Sensory Marketing." March 2015. https://hbr.org/2015/03/the-science-of-sensory-marketing.

Hobbs, Chris. "This is the Ultimate Sacrifice Founders Make - Lloyed Lobo of Boast.AI." *Afternoon "T" Podcast*. February 17, 2021. https://www.youtube.com/watch?v=aeLGOdWo0is.

HubSpot earnings call Q3'22. HubSpot. https://421676.fs1.hubspotusercontent-na1.net/hubfs/421676/Transcript%20-HubSpot%20Q322%20Earnings%20Call.pdf. Published on Nov. 2, 2022.

Huhn, Jessica. "How to Start a Brand Ambassador Program: The Ultimate Guide." *Referral Rock Blog*. June 9, 2023. https://referralrock.com/blog/brand-ambassador-program/.

Ibarra, Amelia. "How To Innovate Faster with Community." *SaaStr*. https://www.saastr.com/how-to-innovate-faster-with-community-insights-from-gitlab/.

Keller, Gary. *The One Thing*. 1st Edition. Portland: Bard Press, 2013.

King, Jude Ph.D. "How Great Leaders Communicate Big Vision So That Others Want To Join In." *Medium*, November 29, 2019. https://medium.com/@Jude.M/how-great-leaders-communicate-big-vision-so-that-others-want-to-join-in-d3296e7ca37e.

Lemkin, Jason and Aaron Ross. *From Impossible to Inevitable*. 2nd edition. Hoboken: Wiley, 2019.

Lemkin, Jason. "The Top 10+ Learnings On How To Build A Large Scale Community." *SaaStr*. https://www.saastr.com/how-did-you-get-started-creating-your-saastr-community-and-how-could-i-get-started-on-making-one-for-a-different-industry/.

Lobo, Lloyed. "11 Steps To Making $250k Hosting A Successful Conference." *Sumo*. November 03, 2021. https://sumo.com/stories/conference-hosting.

Lobo, Lloyed. "The Art & Science of Growth." *Traction Podcast*. March 2, 2021. https://www.youtube.com/watch?v=d7Vaw4U9Osg.

Lloyed Lobo. "Atlassian's Transformational Change Playbook for Exponential Growth with Anu Bharadwaj." *Traction Podcast*. December 22, 2021. https://www.youtube.com/watch?v=6lgrcRIXh5Q.

Lobo, Lloyed. "Building a Media Giant on Top of Your Business To Drive Exponential Growth with Max Altschuler." *Traction Podcast*. August 20, 2021. https://www.youtube.com/watch?v=i_keGu8YIFQ.

Lobo, Lloyed. "The Community Led Growth Playbook - Secrets from Nike, Peloton, Shopify & Duolingo with Sumo Chatterjee." *Traction Podcast*. January 27, 2022. https://www.youtube.com/watch?v=lcYfZmeWDRg.

Lobo, Lloyed. "The Fuel Powering Enduring, Multi-Billion Dollar Businesses with Sarah Tavel, Benchmark." *Traction Podcast*. April 2022. https://open.spotify.com/episode/3YfcoTirIXKmRzYgZhg2qT?si=RBCvXa-FRoGefi5Q43g2fw&nd=1.

Lobo, Lloyed. "HubSpot's $32 Billion Growth Playbook Interview with Kipp Bodnar." *Traction Podcast*. September 9, 2021. https://www.youtube.com/watch?v=1r7nzXQFU9s.

Lobo, Lloyed. "How Noah Kagan Makes $30,000,000+ from AppSumo & Lessons from Starting & Marketing 24 Startups." *Traction Podcast*. July 24, 2020. https://www.youtube.com/watch?v=BbwjYbDs0yQ.

Lomas, Natasha. "GitLab suffers major backup failure after data deletion incident." *TechCrunch*, February 1, 2017. https://techcrunch.com/2017/02/01/gitlab-suffers-major-backup-failure-after-data-deletion-incident/.

Map & Fire. "How To Define Your Brand's Purpose, Vision, Mission, and Values." https://mapandfire.com/field-guide/brand-core-purpose-vision-mission-values/.

MarTechPod. "Monetizing Your Community Marketing Efforts with Lloyed Lobo." https://martechpod.com/episode/ultimate-guide-to-community-led-growth-lloyed-lobo-boast-ai/monetizing-your-community-marketing-efforts-lloyed-lobo-boast-ai/

MarTechPod. "Ultimate Guide to Community-Led Growth." https://martechpod.com/episode/ultimate-guide-to-community-led-growth-lloyed-lobo-boast-ai/.

Mehta, Nick. "The Ultimate Playbook for Creating a New Industry Category." *Traction Conf.* September 17, 2019. https://www.youtube.com/watch?v=QnJ9IZSxiic.

Miller, Zachary. "If you build a community, you won't become a commodity': Boast AI's Lloyed Lobo." *Tearsheet*, February 01, 2022. https://tearsheet.co/podcasts/if-you-build-a-community-you-wont-become-a-commodity-boast-ais-lloyed-lobo/.

Myers, Astasia. "Community is a New Moat!" *Medium*. March 3, 2020. https://medium.com/memory-leak/community-is-the-new-moat-d1678fce7449.

Nestler, Laura. "How Duolingo Scaled to 90 Courses & 300M Users." *Traction Conf.* September 17, 2019. https://www.youtube.com/watch?v=vWUMW6Ovf6o.

Pathways.org. "Sensory." https://pathways.org/topics-of-development/sensory/.

Physician Moms Group (PMG). https://mypmg.com/.

Pine, Joseph, and James Gilmore. *The Experience Economy.* Harvard Business Review Press; Revised edition. Boston, 2019.

Pink, Daniel. *Drive.* New York: Riverhead Books, 2011.

Product Plan. "AARRR Pirate Metrics Framework." https:// www.productplan.com/glossary/aarrr-framework/.

Regaudie, Tiffany. "The Peloton Community Building Playbook." June 28, 2022. https://hashtagpaid.com/ banknotes/the-peloton-community-building-playbook.

Reichheld, Frederick F., and Phil Schefter. "The Economics of E-Loyalty." *Harvard Business Review*, July 10, 2000. https://hbswk.hbs.edu/archive/the-economics-of-e-loyalty.

Rinker, Brian. "What a Founder Learned from His Near-Death Experience with Covid." *San Francisco Business Times*, February 22, 2021. https://www.bizjournals.com/ sanfrancisco/news/2021/02/22/what-founder-learned-from-near-death-covid.html.

Shah, Dharmesh. "The HubSpot Culture Code." HubSpot. June 24, 2021. https://network.hubspot.com/slides/the-hubspot-culture-code-1f8v20t3a.

Silvestre, Monica. "The Definitive Growth Playbook for Building International Communities." Global Growth Accelerator Conference. December 7, 2021. https:// growthblazers.wistia.com/medias/5eqapmzsv7.

Spinks, David. "A Founder's Guide to Community." *Lenny's Newsletter*. November 30, 2021. https://www. lennysnewsletter.com/p/building-community.

Spinks, David. *Business of Belonging.* Hoboken: Wiley, 2021.

Tavel, Sarah. "The Hierarchy of Engagement." *Mind the Product*. September 28, 2018. https://www. mindtheproduct.com/the-hierarchy-of-engagement-by-sarah-tavel/#:~:text=In%20mounting%20loss%2C%20the%20 more,concept%2C%20Sarah%20talks%20about%20 Evernote.

ter Kuile, Casper. *The Power of Ritual*. 1st Edition. San Francisco: HarperOne, 2020.

Warner, Andrew. *Stop Asking Questions*. Chicago: Damn Gravity, 2021.

Yaffe, Daniel. "The State of the Experience Economy." Polaris by AnyRoad. March 17, 2022. https://www.youtube.com/watch?v=u4-aOgxGUak.

ABOUT THE AUTHOR

LLOYED LOBO is an entrepreneur, community builder, speaker, and podcast host. He experienced the power of community firsthand as a young refugee of the Gulf War in Kuwait, where the community came together to evacuate the population to safety. Lloyed is the co-founder of Boast.AI, a fintech platform that provides R&D and Innovation funding to companies. Boast. AI used the community-led growth model to bootstrap to eight figures in revenue. Lloyed is also the co-founder of Traction, a community that is enabling more than a hundred thousand innovators and entrepreneurs to build world-changing companies via connections, content, and capital.